Mended Faith

A Life of Abuse, Pain and Redemption

Mended Faith

A Life of Abuse, Pain and Redemption

CORNELIA JUDE
with CHRIS JONES

NASHVILLE

LONDON • NEW YORK • MELBOURNE • VANCOUVER

Mended Faith

A Life of Abuse, Pain and Redemption

© 2019 Cornelia Jude with Chris Jones

Published in New York, New York, by Morgan James Publishing. Morgan James is a trademark of Morgan James, LLC. www.MorganJamesPublishing.com

The Morgan James Speakers Group can bring authors to your live event. For more information or to book an event visit The Morgan James Speakers Group at www.TheMorganJamesSpeakersGroup.com.

ISBN 9781683508755 paperback
ISBN 9781683508762 eBook
Library of Congress Control Number: 2017918495

Cover Design by:
Christopher Kirk
www.GFSstudio.com

Interior Design by:
Paul Curtis

In an effort to support local communities, raise awareness and funds, Morgan James Publishing donates a percentage of all book sales for the life of each book to Habitat for Humanity Peninsula and Greater Williamsburg.

Get involved today! Visit
www.MorganJamesBuilds.com

To my children, my husband, and the #WolfPack.
None of this would have been possible without your support.

Table of Contents

Foreword 1

Introduction 5

The Cracked Pot 9

Paralyzed 11

Whiskey 17

Master Plan of a Manipulator 23

Just a Phase 33

Beautifully Hurt 39

Dirty 45

Just Let Me Die 53

The Apple Doesn't Fall Far 61

God Sent 73

Don't Send Me to Hell 83

I Choose to Forgive 95

All a Part of God's Plan 101

We Are Never Alone 107

Epilogue 115

Notes 119

Acknowledgements 125

About Cornelia Jude 127

About Chris Jones 129

Foreword

Imagine standing in a courtroom presenting your case before a judge and a jury. You are asked to present evidence as to why you continue to hold on to hope when all seems lost. What evidence will you provide that gives you faith that your life, with all its hurts and tragedies, can be redeemed? The judge asks the bailiff to bring in the evidence you have provided, but there is one problem-your entire defense rests on intangible evidence. Your only evidence consists of that which the jurors cannot see or touch, upon "the substance of things hoped for, the evidence of things not seen."

The jury must decide: Can this invisible evidence really change the outcome of a life? Can nations rise and fall, humanity win or lose, destinies be realized or forfeited, determined entirely by this preposterous evidence? And yet for all those who have been a part of the human experience for any length of time, we must acknowledge that, yes, faith and hope can change the course of events. Throughout history despair has given way to victory as long as hope remained, but without it, defeat proved eminent. This invisible evidence often is the pivotal factor that determines great victory or catastrophic defeat.

This "substance of things hoped for, the evidence of things not seen" called faith is the most powerful force in the universe. It dwarfs the power of an atomic bomb. It can untangle and restore the most twisted and damaged of hearts. No matter how deep the pit of brokenness and despair, faith reaches deeper still. It coaxes us to summon our courage, to take a herculean leap into the unknown, and to choose to forgive.

I am privileged to have experienced an eyewitness account of the marvelous transformation that faith has brought to Conny. Her choice to forgive initiated a powerful domino effect in her own life and in the lives of many others. The invisible substance of faith, mixed with the choice to forgive, detonated the power of God needed to remove the blockade that kept her life from moving forward. An explosion of mercy and grace has once again made "all things new."

I urge you to take Conny's story to heart and to follow her example of choosing to forgive on your own journey to recovery. May I remind you that forgiveness doesn't lessen the evil of the wrong, but simply is a choice for you to rise above it. We are held captive by cell bars forged by our own hands when we choose not to forgive. That choice is your first step in restoring what was lost.

No one can comfort us like the one who has been freed from the same dark valley that we are facing. Renewed hope springs from those who with great empathy state, "I have faced the same darkness and despair that you are facing, and I came through it." This book is that voice.

If you follow in the footsteps of its author, not only will you be restored, but you too will be able "to comfort those in any trouble with the comfort we ourselves receive from God." How marvelous is that? From utter brokenness to a healing balm for others, that is God's plan for you. Others need your story of redemption and I pray that the words of this book will be a part of that process. Hold on to hope!

Pastor Craig Walker
Upward Church

Introduction

"This is my comfort in my affliction, that your word has revived me."

Psalm 119:50

Rape and abuse victims suffer in silence.

I know because I did. Many of you reading this book are, too. According to RAINN, the Rape, Abuse & Incest National Network, only 344 out of every 1,000 sexual assaults are reported. That means nearly 2 out of 3 go unreported. Of those not reported, 20 percent said they maintained their silence for fear of retaliation. The scariest statistic? A combined 15 percent reported that they stayed silent because they didn't think it was important enough to report, or they didn't want to get the perpetrator in trouble.

That's why I chose to disturb my silence and write this book. I wanted to share my life with you to give you the power and courage you need to share your life with others. We owe it to ourselves and each other to draw back the curtains, open the blinds, and let the light shine in. Our stories are important and if by sharing them our abusers have to finally face themselves in the mirror, then that's what has to happen. We are no longer going to be the keepers of their dirty secrets.

I knew how difficult it would be for me to tell my story. My family, who didn't want the secrets exposed, opposed me. Still, I felt led to write this book to help women who like me have suffered in silence dulling their pain with drugs, alcohol, and self-harm. I wanted to show that, through God, we could tap into the power we need to come out from the shadows to become a source of strength and comfort for others in the same way that He comforts us.

God pursued me. He spoke to me through a church sign to get my attention. Like Moses at the burning bush, while it was a terrifying thing to accept, I answered the call after many days of wrestling with God's calling. I hope that if you feel the gentle prodding of God asking you to come forward and share your story with others that you will. We need more women to confront and to disturb the silence that surrounds sexual abuse. I can't promise that it will be an easy road. It hasn't been for me, but it has been worth it.

The reality for me struck one night as I was talking to my pastors. They convinced me that something positive was going to come from me opening up about my life. Prior to that, I didn't see anything good in being raped, physically and mentally abused, being abandoned, or falling prey to drugs and alcohol, or self-mutilation. I'm not sure that anyone could have. Yet, when I talked to my pastors they said, "You know you could make a big difference." I have come to see and know that God loves using people like me-an everyday, ordinary woman. But that's the way it's always been, right. In Acts 4:23, it says:

"When [The Pharisees] saw the courage of Peter and John and realized that they were unschooled, ordinary men, they were astonished and they took note that these men had been with Jesus."

I have an opportunity with this book to show others the love of Christ through what I have suffered, endured, and overcome. I don't expect you to just start talking about your pain openly. I have tried for many years to talk about it but the words wouldn't even form on my lips. Every time I wanted the words to come out, I got choked up. So, I wrote about it, and maybe you could, too. Keep a journal; write down your thoughts and feelings. The act of getting it out on paper will slowly help you to begin the process of talking about it-even if it's just to a close, trusted friend. You also have to know yourself and identify your limits-how much can you write about it? How long can you talk about it? Opening up will send old memories flooding back in explosive detail. Handle your heart with care. Your heart is the wellspring of life.

I found it most difficult to talk with my husband and kids about my abuse. I was so afraid that all I had endured and struggled with would hurt them. That may be a concern for you, too. My kids and I share such a deep emotional attachment that I feared they would be hurt over all that had happened to me. It's a genuine concern that crossed my mind and one that all survivors in significant relationships worry about.

As I began to open up and allow God to heal my heart and mind, prayer became a central focus for me. As strange as this may sound, I included my rapist in my prayers. He was always on my mind. He's been on my mind more than anybody else in this world. He has also visited my dreams more than anybody else. I decided that through prayer, I was going to break up those thoughts that were hindering my entire life. It wasn't until I publicly prayed for him that my connection to him broke.

Now, I want to be a beacon of hope for those who have to deal with the repercussions of being sexually abused yet made to feel like victims. No one believed me for many years. Maybe no one believes you either. Within the pages of this book, I'm going to tell you more about my life and how God has changed my perspective on what I've lived through. I want you to know what a difference it makes and that everything that has happened in our lives-even our hurts-is for a reason. You may not understand why just yet but know that God does, and He has a plan to use those experiences to make you stronger and more useful in changing the world around you. Look, I was once a skeptic, too. I didn't believe that God could take away, let alone heal, the hurts that I carried with me every day, but He did. Like me, you too will have to learn to let go, and my story will show you how I did that. I am a victim no more and when we're done, neither will you be. It's time to exchange depression, shame, and victimhood for forgiveness, grace, and a crown.

Prologue

The Cracked Pot

"I'm hard on myself, so I'm working on shifting perspective toward self-acceptance, with all my flaws and weaknesses."

Gwyneth Paltrow

A water bearer in India had two large pots, one hung on each end of a pole, which she carried across her neck.

One of the pots had a crack in it. While the other pot was perfect, and always delivered a full portion of water at the end of the long walk from the stream to the mistress's house, the cracked pot arrived only half full.

For a full two years this went on daily, with the bearer delivering only one-and-a-half pots full of water to her master's house.

The perfect pot was proud of its accomplishments, perfect to the end for which it was made. But the poor cracked pot was ashamed of its own imperfection, and miserable that it was able to accomplish only half of what it had been made to do.

After two years of what it perceived to be a bitter failure, it spoke to the water bearer one day by the stream: "I am ashamed of myself, and I want to apologize to you."

"Why?" asked the bearer. "What are you ashamed of?"

"I have been able, for these past two years, to deliver only half my load because this crack in my side causes water to leak out all the way back to your mistress's house. Because of my flaws, you have to do all of this work, and you don't get full value from your efforts," the pot said.

The water bearer felt sorry for the old cracked pot, and in her compassion, she said, "As we return to the mistress's house, I want you to notice the beautiful flowers along the path."

Indeed, as they went up the hill, the old cracked pot took notice of the sun warming the beautiful wild flowers on the side of the path, and this cheered it some.

But at the end of the trail, it still felt bad because it had leaked out half its load, and so again it apologized to the bearer for its failure.

The bearer said to the pot, "Did you notice that there were flowers only on your side of the path, but not on the other pot's side? That's because I have always known about your flaw, and I took advantage of it. I planted flower seeds on your side of the path, and every day while we walk back from the stream, you've watered them.

"For two years, I have been able to pick these beautiful flowers to decorate my mistress's table. Without you being just the way you are, she would not have this beauty to grace her house."

Chapter 1

Paralyzed

It was late summer in Germany and still pretty warm outside. I was wearing a yellow-green and blue pastel dress. I must have been 3 or 4 years old. The balcony door was open, and I could see the bright yellow sun setting between the high-rises. My parents had company that evening. At the time, I wasn't sure if the man was a distant cousin or just a family friend, but there was beer and whiskey on the table and cigarette smoke filled the room. I loved the smell of that mixture as a child. That meant that there would be music and I loved how silly my dad danced. When my mom danced, she liked to swing her arms from side to side. That made me giggle.

The stranger-a short man who had mid-length long wavy dark hair, a beard, and brown eyes-wasn't there just for the company of my parents. He had on a T-shirt and jean shorts that showed off his hairy legs. He had straight yellow teeth and spoke with a funny dialect that now I recognize as one from possibly Hamburg. He started inching uncomfortably close to me, stroking my little arms and rubbing my tiny shoulders. No one except for my dad had ever touched me like that before and when he did, it never felt weird. The touch of this man felt gross to me. It wasn't like the innocent and loving touch of my father.

I did what most children my age would do-I hid. I moved out of his reach and crawled under the dining room table. I wanted to still be near my parents because I liked to watch them have fun, but I had to get away from the man. Looking up from my place on the floor, all I could see were everyone's legs and feet, but that was OK. I was still a part of the party. As I giggled along with the adult's jokes, I felt something rubbing on my leg. I tried to move, but there was not much room under the table with everyone else seated there. I felt his toes on my thigh and I knew that I needed to move, but I was stuck. As he started to move my panties to the side, a feeling of paralysis came over me. I wanted to move away but couldn't. He placed his toe into my private parts and began sliding his foot back and forth. I hated the feeling. My mom called out to me, "Cornelia!" I jumped up, and, out of shock and fear, I peed on myself a little.

I came from under the table. "I can't believe how nosy she is," my mom said. "She will pee on herself before she would miss any adult conversation."

My mom made me go wash up and change. At that moment, I put on a pair of pants. After what had just happened, I now hated dresses. Once I got dressed, I went back to the party to say goodnight to everyone. The man gave me 5 Deutsche Marks (nearly $3) and told me to buy all of the candy that I wanted. He called me "angel" and as I walked away with my money, I thought, *Maybe he is not that creepy after all.*

* * *

"If anyone causes one of these little ones-those who believe in me-to stumble, it would be better for them if a large millstone were hung around their neck and they were thrown into the sea."

Mark 9:42

God loves innocence. When Jesus was making his triumphal entry days before his crucifixion, it was the children who recognized him, waving their palm branches and singing in the streets, "Hosanna to the Son of David! Blessed is he who comes in the name of the Lord!" God loves children because, as kids, we haven't been tainted and corrupted by sin. We are beautiful souls that are allowed to run free, to imagine, and to marvel at the world God has placed around us.

At some point, the veil is removed, and our innocent view of the world is shattered. Sometimes it's the natural progression of childhood and seeing things like the suffering and death of a grandparent or other loved one, the loss of a pet, or hurtful words from classmates or those we care about. Other times, it's the sin of others that directly takes away our innocence.

Jesus said that those who harm children-his little ones-would be better off cast into the sea with a large millstone around their necks. To give you a perspective, let's look at what that looks like.

A millstone was a tool used for grinding wheat or grain in ancient Israel. A mill consisted of two heavy, flat, circular stones, with one resting on the other. The lower stone was stationary. The upper stone was rotated with a handle around a peg that was fastened into the lower stone and passed through a funnel-shaped hole in the upper one. Grain was poured into the funnel and then ground between the stones, which created flour. Small mills were worked by hand, but a donkey turned larger ones because of their size and weight. So, when Jesus says a large millstone, he is talking about the latter. Those millstones were approximately 53 inches in diameter, 8 inches thick, and had a hole 13 square inches wide-the size of a monster-truck tire. This is what Jesus said would be better fit around the neck of someone who causes the innocent to stumble. Replace the charm at the end of your necklace with one of those and you have a clear visual of how much innocence means to Jesus.

That night in my own home, my trust was stolen. I will never know why that man decided to do what he did to me, but it was an event that would change my entire life. My parents didn't know it happened. It was our secret. The worst part as I share this story with you is the hindsight that he paid me to keep quiet. He bribed me. And isn't it always like that? When we are violated in our most intimate places, we are told to keep quiet. We may be offered something in exchange or threatened. So we don't speak up, but close up. We feel the paralysis in our speech when we try to talk about it. And sadly, we wonder who may judge us for the actions that others have done to us. It's not enough that we live in a culture where victims shoulder the blame for being abused. We are often questioned and made to feel more shame and ridicule than those who have abused us. This has to change. Our words and testimony must become the millstones that hang on the necks of those who have robbed us of our innocence. If not, our suffering in silence will cause us to waste away.

In Christ, we have a loving advocate who will stand with us when others may not. God is in the business of restoring our innocence. He has the power to cleanse us of the pain of the past and renew us from the inside out. In Psalm 18, David says, "He is the God who avenges me, who subdues nations under me." If God could subdue nations under David and deliver him from the harmful hand of King Saul, he can restore and renew us. He wants to.

When was your innocence lost? Do you remember how it made you feel? I didn't like wearing dresses again for many years afterward. Loss of innocence changes us. What we love we separate ourselves from because of the painful reminders. My prayer is that you will allow God to work in that situation for you and remove those blocks. It wasn't the fault of my dresses. The dress was an easy avenue for him to gain access to me. Rather than blame objects, or places, or songs, which we all sometimes do, let's bring the person who harmed us before Jesus in prayer. When we find our comfort in Christ and hold our abusers accountable before God, we can begin to enjoy many of the beautiful things God has provided for us.

I pray that you will ask God to help you while you walk down the path toward restoring your innocence, and that, through Him, you will let go of the hurt that carrying this pain has held over you for so long. Let God be your avenger while you dance in the joy of being free and renewed with the spirit of a child.

Chapter 2

Whiskey

I don't like the smell of whiskey and smoke anymore.

My parent's constant yelling and screaming at one another made me want out of the door of our second-floor apartment. Even at 8 years old, there were just some things I couldn't get used to. But there was my dad, looking out of the window of our apartment, yelling at my mom, who said a few words back to him before disappearing into the rain. Their spats typically revolved around my dad always being late or his constant drinking. So, I went to the playground with two of my friends.

After walking back to our building, I walked up the flight of stairs leading to our apartment. I could hear my father's loud music from behind the door. When I pushed it open, the smell of cigar smoke and whiskey was an unwelcome greeting. The scent was stronger and the smoke thicker than usual. The house was dark except for the flickering of a red candle on the dining-room table. The songs are recognizable now-old favorites of mom and dad, only I couldn't see either of them. I made my way into the dining room where I could see my dad, his blue eyes staring at the fat candle on the table. When his Peter Maffay record was playing, he was usually dancing around and being silly. But not that night; that night, he was hurting-badly. My only guess is that my mother was off with her new boyfriend, who at one time was a friend of my father's.

I pulled out a chair across the table from my dad and sat crookedly on the seat.

"I'm sorry," he muttered.

I wanted to hug him and tell him how much I love him, but instead, I continued to listen to the song.

I looked away for a moment, and then I heard my father dragging air through his teeth and I could smell the singeing of his hairs as he dug his cigar into the name "Renate" on his arm.

All I could do was watch him burn away the rejection and pain from my mother. I didn't ask any questions. I couldn't stop him. I watched and wondered how many whiskeys it took to dull the pain of using his cigar to erase an unwanted memory.

* * *

"When Jesus climbed out of the boat, a man possessed by an evil spirit came out from a cemetery to meet him… Day and night he wandered among the burial caves and in the hills, howling and cutting himself with sharp stones."

Mark 5:2, 5

Can you image the rejection and pain this man must have felt? He was shackled and subdued with chains in caves meant to house the dead, away from those he loved and knew. He was unstable, and they feared him. The inner demons that spoke to him and influenced him drove him to howling in pain and cutting himself, the body and image that was made in the likeness of God his creator, with sharp stones.

I watched as my father tried to burn away the pain of losing my mother's affection with his hot cigar. He couldn't bear to look upon himself and see her name etched on his skin. And though he eventually was successful at burning it off, it left a permanent scar.

My father's inability to cope with pain wasn't much different than that of the man in the cave. Neither is the pain of many people in the world today. Maybe we aren't burning our skin with cigars or cutting ourselves with stones, but we self-destruct when we turn to drugs, abuse alcohol, and when we engage in risky behavior to take away the pain. We are taught to hate pain. We don't want to feel it. We don't want to face it. I didn't and neither did my father. Worst of all, we do it in the dark- alone and isolated. These inner demons we face only want to isolate us, destroy us, and permanently keep us separated from relationships with those we love and with God. From dark places of despair, we cry. We don't think anyone can understand our pain. We don't think anyone will love us through our pain. The enemy whispers cleverly crafted lies into our ear night and day hoping to draw us further and further from those we love and from God. If they only knew what I did? we think. If they only knew what happened to me, they wouldn't love me, we utter.

We forget that pain and suffering are universal, that rejection and hopelessness are human conditions that all people endure at one time or another. But we are loved and we are understood because despite the lies we listen to and believe from the enemy, others have gone through pain. Consider Paul's words to the Corinthian church:

> *"Praise be to the God and Father of our Lord Jesus Christ, the Father of compassion and the God of all comfort, who comforts us in all our troubles, so that we can comfort those in any trouble with the comfort we ourselves receive from God. For just as we share abundantly in the sufferings of Christ, so also our comfort abounds through Christ."*

Isn't that beautiful? Our suffering is created to be a comfort to others. As my father suffered, I'm sure he wasn't thinking, I'll endure this with all joy because I want to help someone else with their suffering. I doubt that any of us do. It comes after the experience and lesson, after we have an encounter with Christ.

In the tomb, Jesus approached the man upon hearing his name called. Jesus gets personal with him. "What is your name?" he asks. Jesus doesn't judge him. Jesus doesn't question his self-destructive habits. He doesn't get upset at the condition of the man's heart. He doesn't even ask him why he's harming himself. He just meets him where he is and, in his love, compassion, and wisdom, addresses the problem. "Come out of the man, you evil spirit," he says. Then the spirits depart. The man's sanity and heart are restored, and he began to share the good news of Christ.

* * *

Self-destructive habits, like those of my father and of the man in the cave, stem from us not understanding how much we mean to God. It wasn't until the man had an encounter with Jesus that he was able to find genuine love and see his complete value. He saw himself as Jesus did-a complete person worthy of love despite what he had done to himself as few as five minutes earlier. We are worthy. I am worthy of the unconditional love and acceptance of Jesus and so are you.

What challenges are you facing that have left you feeling hopeless? Which self-destructive habits have you used to numb your pain? What or where is your cave, your place of isolation? From whom do you feel rejection? For my father, it was my mother. No matter how we feel, it's time for us to come out. The invitation of Christ is a loving embrace and a clean slate.

Rejection hurts. If you have felt the rejection of family and friends over your life choices, or your response to pain, setbacks, and trauma as I have, just look upward to Jesus. The Scriptures promise time and again that if we seek him we will find him. He is waiting. We have to come out of our cave, crying out his name.

Chapter 3

Master Plan of a Manipulator

I was diagnosed with asthma at 8 years old. At first, my doctor thought it was psychological and related to trauma; my twin cousins died in a fire. They finally figured out that it was unrelated and began to treat me. By the time I reached 12 years old, it was severe to the point that I had at least three hospital stays each year for as long as two weeks at a time.

Having to stay in hospitals for treatment was boring. Some days my friends would come and hang out with me at the hospital. The doctors would pump me full of breathing treatments, connect me to IVs, and I would have tons of blood work done, which was the worst. As I got older, I welcomed the stays because I would be safe and out of my house.

My dad visited when he could, which was usually once or twice per week, and I loved it when he came. He brought in foods I loved to eat—cucumbers, carrots, cauliflower, grapes, and tangerines—so that I wasn't stuck with the less than desirable hospital food. I remember how it would hurt to breathe and how I was allergic to what felt like everything on earth—dust, dogs, cats, horses, grass, and cleaning supplies. Asthma kept me from the fun things I enjoyed.

As an asthmatic child, I always panicked, not knowing when it's going to creep up on me. As long as I had my inhaler on me I did OK, but the second I realized that I didn't have it, panic pushed me right into an attack. I would lie on the floor and concentrate on my breathing. Listening to the wheezing helped me calm down and I would stay like that until someone found an inhaler for me. I absolutely hated the helpless feeling.

On top of frequently being sick, my parents got divorced. I didn't get to see my brother regularly anymore and I hated being away from him. We used to always be together, but now he moved in with our dad and I lived with our mom. The whole situation didn't help with my sickness either.

During this time, my mom started seeing someone new, a man named Rolf. My brother wasn't crazy about him. While he seemed nice at first and was always playful toward me, he was 11 years younger than my mom. He wasn't like her old boyfriend, who my brother and I did like, who eventually left. I think he got tired of my dad beating on him. It was an awkward situation since he was my dad's friend at one time. I remember one Sunday, we were on our way to our grandmother's house when my dad spotted his car driving down the street—and the chase was on! Dad almost ran him off the road before he stopped, pulled him out of the car, and whooped him in the middle of the street. Another time my dad beat him up in the bedroom and then throughout every room in the house.

* * *

In the first twelve years of my life, my family moved seven times. While I missed my friends, it was only a 20-minute drive from my new house back to where I lived before. My new school wasn't too bad, I did like my teacher, but it was hard for me to keep up with all the extra work since I was constantly ill. My teacher, Mrs. Melcher, made sure that she kept me on track with my grades. They were not the best of grades, but I never failed a class or quiz. I had gotten so sick once that my mom took me out of school and admitted me to a clinic for six weeks, which turned into eight weeks because all the treatments didn't help. My mom always did what she could to make sure that I had the proper care.

On one occasion where I fell sick with asthma, my mom had to work. We had been living in our new house for close to three months from what I remember. Her boyfriend was living with us and she asked him to stay home to take care of me. He picked up food for us, and we watched a movie. He took really good care of me, and I felt safe.

I fell asleep on the couch and woke up to him carrying me to what I thought was my bedroom until I realized that I was in my mom's bed. He told me that my mom had instructed him to make sure that I used my inhaler and to put vapor rub on my back and chest. I told him that I could rub my own chest, but he could help me with my back since there was no way for me to reach. *Did my mom really tell him to rub my chest?* I thought. Maybe I shouldn't be uncomfortable if she instructed him to do so. I lifted my T-shirt a little. My hair was up in a loose ponytail. He started covering my back with the vapor rub using only one hand, which almost covers my whole back. He asked me to turn over and told me I would feel better sooner if he also put it on my chest. As he started rubbing my chest, I realized that it didn't feel like my mom's touch—she would rub the vapor rub quickly between her hands and then use fast strokes to massage it into my skin. *He is doing it wrong,* I thought. He started applying it on my chest in a slow, circular motion with his hands easing toward my stomach. "You don't need to do that," I said. "Shh… you will feel better," he replied. He slid his hand into my sweats and inched his finger closer to my vagina. *This is uncomfortable,* I thought. I wanted to jump up, but there was this stuck feeling—a locking of my body that I hadn't felt since I was four. I can feel the yellow-toothed man's toe again, pushing against my privates, hurting me, and then seeing his face as he gave me money to buy candy and keep quiet. My head started spinning, and I felt sick. As he sat on the edge of my mom's bed, a hot, stinging sensation hit my vagina and he's babbling things that I didn't understand. That was the last thing I remembered.

I woke up to a cold, wet towel on my forehead. It was about 2 or 3 a.m. My mom was sitting on the edge of the bed holding my hand. Her boyfriend told her I had been fighting a fever, but that he gave me meds and rubbed me down with vapor rub. She was happy that he took such good care of me. He insisted that I stay in their bed so they could keep an eye on me all night.

* * *

The next day, I woke up in my mom's bed; I could hear her vacuuming the living room. As I lay there just staring, thoughts racing through my head about what had happened that night, I was fighting my mind hoping it was all just a dream, but it wasn't. It was not a dream. My mom's boyfriend has crossed a boundary. I started to wonder, *What if I just tell my mom?* Is she going to hate me? She loves him so much, even when he calls her names she plays it off. Would she believe me? I don't know what to do or where to turn. Would anyone believe me?

Since I was afraid to tell my mom what had happened, he had me right where he wanted me. From that point, he started coming into my room frequently. He could tell that I was too ashamed or too afraid to tell my mom and, even if I did, I knew that he could wiggle his way out of it. That's what he always did. As he came into my room unwelcomed, it was hard for me to open my eyes and look at him. I tried many times. I just sat or lied there motionless. And when he pushed his hand down my shirt or into my pants, I froze. He made me feel dirty and when he finished—and as odd as this sounds—I would scratch my skin until it bled, and it felt surprisingly good.

Now that home was no longer safe, I started staying out of the house as much as I could. I would be at the park, or at a friend's house. My mom didn't seem to mind whether I was home or not. Sometimes I was gone for two to three days at a time only to come home to change clothes when no one was there. When I did come home, my mom and I would fight over things that Rolf did and blamed me for—like the house being dirty. All she cared about was his happiness; I knew the deal. At night, I had nightmares. She would tell me each morning after that Rolf came and checked on me. She was clueless as to what he was really doing. She worked so hard that she would come home and fall into a deep sleep after working so many hours. She never felt him leaving their bed and, despite how strange it would be for him to shower in the middle of the night after leaving my room. He had OCD, so my mom thought nothing of it. All she wanted to know is if my nightmares were because I was messing with the witch board again. There was a phase when my friends and I used an Ouija board to talk to the dead. It scared me so much that I didn't sleep for weeks. On the contrary, I wasn't messing with anything, I was being messed with—and I wanted badly to tell her so many times.

* * *

"In the course of time, Amnon son of David fell in love with Tamar, the beautiful sister of Absalom son of David. Amnon became so obsessed with his sister Tamar that he made himself ill. She was a virgin, and it seemed impossible for him to do anything to her."

2 Samuel 13:1-2

Lust can make a person do things they know they shouldn't do and the outcome is worse than the fantasy they had in mind. For men like my mom's boyfriend, it doesn't just happen. With me, he was friendly at first. He played around with me and made it seem like it was about having fun and getting to know me. He built my trust and my guard was down. My mom wasn't worried about him with me either. This is what's called grooming; when a sexual predator establishes trust with his victim beneath the noses of their unsuspecting parents.

Forensic psychiatrist Dr. Michael Welner, who has worked on the cases of Andrea Yates and Elizabeth Smart, defines grooming as "the process by which an offender draws a victim into a sexual relationship and maintains that relationship in secrecy. The shrouding of the relationship is an essential feature of grooming."

I was an easy target for Rolf. My mother worked long hours and sometimes deep into the night. My brother lived with my father. That just left us alone for long amounts of time. Welner says predators like my mom's boyfriend tend to "target a victim by sizing up the child's vulnerability—emotional neediness, isolation, and lower self-confidence. Children with less parental oversight are more desirable prey."

He chose the most vulnerable time to begin his molestation of me—while I was sick, defenseless, and alone. He took on a role of trust, caring for me under the guidance and permission of my mother, and decided to make his move. Who knows how long he thought about making that sort of move, but he found the right time. Then he continued once he knew I was unable to speak up and advocate for myself.

Amnon, whose sister suspected nothing (why should she have?) pretended to be ill. He requested the care of his sister to nurse him back to health and his father, King David, granted it. When she entered his space, and was fully within his grip, he seized the opportunity to act on his desires and raped her. He took advantage of his close relationship to remove her defenses. And what happened after he got what he wanted from her? He found her disgusting in his sight and he wanted nothing to do with her ever again. In reality, you can see his conscience couldn't handle what he did and the thing he thought he had wanted so badly he showed contempt for. He projected his shame onto his sister, causing her to feel his icy cold rejection. His desires meant everything, and her life meant nothing.

My mother's boyfriend acted in the same manner toward me. Once he began to inappropriately touch me and rape me, he treated me with the same kind of contempt that Amnon treated his sister, Tamar. And I, too, felt the shame of rejection. In the Bible, it says that after choosing to follow his lust-filled desires, which lead him to rape his sister, that "Amnon hated her with intense hatred. In fact, he hated her more than he had loved her." Then he made her get up, get out, and he locked the door behind her leaving her to deal with the shame that he had brought on her. When we last hear of Tamar, she lived the rest of her days with her brother Absalom as a desolate woman, never to know love, marry, or have children. That was the penalty in those days for the loss of virginity. By no fault of her own, she was left to bear the burden of Amnon's choice—his sin against her body.

Welner says that once sex abuse is occurring, offenders commonly use secrecy and blame to maintain the child's continued participation and silence. For me, that's what it became. He called me names, shamed me, and kept me quiet. Like Tamar, I felt broken, used, and undesirable. I was left with nightmares and a downward spiral of negative coping mechanisms for many years to come.

Grooming is subtle. It looks like play. Depending on the relationship, the conspiring adult wants to appear like a father figure, a grandfather, an uncle, or a fun, older-brother type. For the unsuspecting child, it's great. It's a break from the family members they feel don't understand them or relate to them. Our kids today are vulnerable. I'm not saying that every stepparent, significant other, blended family non-related sibling, or other close relationship will end in grooming and sexual abuse, but wisdom says to keep your eyes open and be involved in the life of your child. Isolation is how these things happen but having regular conversations and giving your child an opportunity to speak openly can protect them from predatory relationships.

Chapter 4

Just a Phase

I started sniffing glue when I was 12 years old. No, not the typical $1 bottle of white glue that you can find at Walmart or Target. I was sniffing wallpaper glue out of a bag. I watched another girl who huffed and after seeing how totally relaxed it made her afterward, I was convinced to try it, too. Glue was a cheap high—which didn't last long at all—and it was easy to buy at hardware stores. We would mix it with water, stir it, and put it in a plastic shopping bag. Then we would go to the park and share the bag. I sniffed it for a while, but since I had asthma, I would end up in the hospital because the scent of the glue would trigger my asthma attacks.

I moved on to LSD at 13. It came on a small piece of paper that looked like a sticker. That was a one-and-done drug for me. It pulled me into a different type of world—full of strange hallucinations—and I couldn't break free of the high. When I tried it, my friend and I were on a soccer field where nobody ever went and there was a little playground there. It was our hangout spot. There was a guy who taught us the best way to use. He said we should cut the paper into four pieces and then take it, which we did. I placed it on my tongue and let it dissolve. At first it was hilarious because my friend's face started looking funny and I laughed for a while, but then I just felt stuck in my hallucination. The high lasted a very long time and each time I started feeling as though I was coming out of it, I was thrown back into hallucinations. It took me two days to get over it.

I decided to try cocaine, but not because I wanted to get high. It was given to me for a toothache. I was told to rub it on my gums, which I did, and didn't get terribly high from it. I just remember feeling all over the place and having a lot of energy. I tried it a couple more times—smoked and inhaled—but it just didn't do anything for me, and it was expensive. When I wanted to use, money never became a problem. I always had access from somewhere, whether I got it from my parents or other places.

I also smoked hash at one point. Drugs helped me cope with depression. I'd just find myself some drugs and it would momentarily take away the pain. It was heartbreaking to watch people who I was acquainted with overdosing on harder drugs like heroin. I never tried heroin for that very reason. Losing friends to that may have saved my life.

Looking back at my life, all I wanted was for someone to protect me. Instead, I turned to drugs to numb the pain. Using never really made my pain go away. Nothing goes away until you deal with the issue. That's hindsight though, right? The drugs and alcohol helped me to forget and to feel good when I used them; drugs ultimately end in two scenarios, we either quit using them or they kill us. There are no other options.

I lost a lot of friends to drugs because they didn't know how or when to quit. When I was seventeen, I became pregnant and that was the end of it for me. I just knew I had to protect that child no matter what, so I quit using. Pregnancy saved my life, and I believe it saved my brother's life, too. He also abused drugs as a teenager. Toward the end of my pregnancy, I had a scare that hospitalized me. While there, my brother promised that he would turn his life around if I didn't die. I recovered, and my brother never touched drugs again. I lost my baby that day but saved my brother's life.

* * *

I was also 12 years old when I started drinking. My friends and I had to be creative to get alcohol, but even still, most places really didn't check ID. I started drinking beer and wine at first, and then it got heavier. I drank brandy for a while because it was cheap. At 14, I would go to adult nightclubs; getting in was no problem because I looked so much older than I really was. People bought me drinks all the time. Some nights I would drink so much that I'd wake up having no idea where I was, if I had slept with somebody, what I did that night, or what was going on. At my lowest point, I was drinking a six-pack of beer a day and if someone else had something to drink, I'd have whatever they were drinking, too. The alcohol by volume in Germany is much higher than in standard beer in the U.S., so it was easy to get drunk. But once I drank a few beers, it was really hard for me to say no to more. We would drink after school. We would meet men at the park to drink. We had nothing better to do. Besides fun, I was drinking to forget my home life. I would go from having a really good time when I was drinking to having to go home and that was depressing.

My family knew I was drinking and no one cared enough to stop me. They just allowed it to happen. I was drunk and out of my mind at 12 years old and no one had a problem with that. They knew about the drugs as well. Thinking back on that, it hurts. I deserved to have someone fight for me—every child does—but no one did.

* * *

"Suppose one of you has a hundred sheep and loses one of them. Doesn't he leave the ninety-nine in the open country and go after the lost sheep until he finds it?"

Luke 15:4

It's often said that sheep are dumb. We usually call people who follow the crowd, an unpopular opinion, or political positions we don't like sheep. Contrary to what you think, sheep are actually intelligent animals. Their smarts rank with cows and are just below pigs. Sheep follow their instincts much like we follow our emotions and they tend to run away and get lost when they're afraid.

That was me. Lost not because I wanted to be lost, but because I was afraid. I ended up in the wrong fold of sheep for a number of years. I got drunk and high because I wanted friends. I wanted a way out of my pain. I wanted to forget how bad it felt to come home to a family that didn't care about me and to a man who came into my room unwelcome for his pleasure.

Had I not gotten pregnant, who knows how far I would have gone. I didn't know then that I needed a savior. I needed Jesus, and even though I didn't know it. He knew. It took him over 20 years of hiking the open country (as the Bible says) to find this lost sheep. But he found me and pulled me into his flock.

> *"The Lord is not slow in keeping his promise, as some understand slowness. Instead he is patient with you, not wanting anyone to perish, but everyone to come to repentance."*

2 Peter 3:9

I feel blessed to know that despite all the harm and self-destruction I brought upon myself, God didn't let me meet my end. It could have easily happened with a bad trip on LSD that first time, overdoing it with the glue, alcohol poisoning, or even cocaine. Time after time, God spared my life and I had no idea. I just thought I was lucky to have not died. I see what God has brought me through and the message he has given me to share, there was no luck. He wanted me to come to repentance so that I could share my story with you.

I'm sure if you think back on your own life and the ways in which you tried to drown out your own pain and sorrows, you can see God's patience with you. You can see a clear pathway from your pain to your purpose. The things you endured that you can now speak of and share with others.

Thinking back to being a wild teenager and wishing that someone thought me worthy to fight for, it wasn't my mother, my father, or anyone else advocating for my life, but it was Jesus. At the right hand of God, he petitioned the Father for me and he chased me down for decades until he found me. That's what a good shepherd does.

Chapter 5

Beautifully Hurt

I started cutting myself at about 13 or 14 years old. The first time, I carved my arm with a broken piece of glass that I found while I was at the park hanging out with some homeless people earlier that day. I don't know why I decided to start cutting. I picked up a broken bottle from the ground one day at the park and the glass cut my finger. There was no pain, just warm blood that looked pure and beautiful. I remember just staring down and watching the blood running down my finger. I took that piece of glass home with me and dragged it across my forearm that day in my bathroom. That was the beginning.

* * *

The first time I truly cut, I was at home alone. I went inside of my bathroom, locked the door, and sat on the floor with my legs crossed leaning against the bathtub, still numb from drinking. I sliced the glass onto my arm and watched the blood run. It was warm as a small red stream and it raced down my arm. Once I realized what I had done, I was scared. I thought, *Whoa. What did I just do? Why am I cutting myself?* Though I freaked myself out, I couldn't stop. I didn't cut again for a week or two after my first cutting experience, but after that, I started cutting daily.

When I cut, I didn't feel any pain—I did it for the blood. It always felt good. I cannot recall seeing anyone do it ever before and I never wanted to hurt myself, just dull the pain I felt inside from being abused. There was one time when I cut so deeply that my arm bled more than I thought it would. I'm not sure how deep I cut; it was enough for me to have to wrap some toilet tissue around my arm and put pressure on the gash to stop the bleeding.

Cutting is addictive and, once you begin, it's not easy to end. To this day, sometimes I think of cutting myself when I have rough days. It's a tension reliever—a way to regain control. My left arm has more scars than my right arm, but then there were times when I would cut my legs, which were easier for me to hide. The cutting would get worse the more my stepdad came into my room at night. I would take a lot of showers after that, and when the water ran into my cuts, they would burn.

I broke a glass at home intentionally for the sharp-edged shards. It was always very thin glass. German beer glasses were perfect because they were really thin, and I would break one for me to carry around. Using such thin pieces of glass is how I came up with the idea to switch to razor blades; they were thinner, the cuts were cleaner, and I bled more with less effort.

While I liked to hide in the bathroom to cut, sometimes I did cut in my bedroom. That was until the padlock that my brother installed on my door to protect me from my mom's boyfriend's nightly visits was taken off the door. One day, while peeking through my bedroom window, my mom's boyfriend caught me smoking in my room. Cutting in my bedroom wasn't an option after that. Some of my friends knew that I was cutting. Some people in my family did, too. My mom didn't at first though. Once when I was 14, she saw my bare arms completely by accident when she walked into my bedroom. She yelled, "What is this?" as she continued to chastise me, saying that I was an out-of-control teenager and that I was losing it. She ran out of my room and told everyone about it and they told her that I needed professional help. Sadly enough, no one tried to help me. It was one of those knee-jerk reactions of hers where she would yell and then she would get over it. She was always at work and didn't really have time for me, so she would just say, "Stop it!" and then she would move on. She wasn't one to sit me down and say, "Let's dig deeper. Let's see what's going on with you." I was just out of control to her, determined to do whatever I wanted to do.

Until that day, I was really good at hiding my cutting. I was good at hiding everything I did from everyone. I felt alone. My mom didn't seem to care either way. It didn't make a difference. I would come home at 3 in the morning, and no one would question where I had been. Sometimes I was gone for a few days at a time and no one was ever concerned enough to find out where I was, what I had been doing, or if I had gone to school. Nothing!

What's weird is that despite cutting with razor blades, I had tried to kill myself four times but never with a razor blade against my wrists. I had every opportunity but cutting wasn't about suicide; it was about comfort, like a safe place for me. It was the only safety I had.

I did stop cutting altogether when I was probably 16 or 17. I had a boyfriend and I was finally away from my stepdad and my mom. I left home and stayed with him and his family.

* * *

"Or do you not know that your body is a temple of the Holy Spirit within you, whom you have from God? You are not your own, for you were bought with a price. So glorify God in your body."

1 Corinthians 6:19-20

To this day, I still have scars on my arms and a couple of them on my legs. They're very faint, for which I'm truly thankful. But they are a constant reminder of how lost and hurt I was as a young teenage girl. I knew some people who had the really thick scars.

I don't know if you've ever cut before or know someone who cuts, but it's a coping mechanism. It allows us to release anxiety and stress and still feel like we are in charge when our world is spiraling out of control, or we feel under the thumb of an abusive or inappropriate relationship. I cut for nearly four years to deal with the sexual abuse and trauma I lived through every day in my home. When I look at my faint scars, I have reminders of this dark and painful time and how I tried to self-sooth.

I know it seems cliché, but God cares about and feels our pain. In 1 Peter 5:7, the Bible says, "Cast all your anxiety on him because he cares for you." We live in a world riddled with anxiety. In fact, studies have said that 1 in 6 Americans take psychiatric drugs to manage anxiety and depression. That's a lot of people medicating their pain. While there is nothing wrong with seeking professional help and managing with medication, there is a spiritual part of us that also needs to let God in to work with those treatments. If not, we can feel some level of relief, but the lasting change won't take place. For me, it was accepting what had happened, and learning to forgive myself for what I had done to myself from within my place of pain and hurt. No matter what we do or how we try to cover pain, mask pain, or defer pain, it does not go away. We have to do as Peter instructs and cast all of our pain, anxiety, fear, and hurts onto Jesus and let him do the good work in us as we walk in faith. The scars he bears have healed me far better than the scars I created—and he can do the same for you.

Chapter 6

Dirty

If you've been sexually abused, you know the icky feeling of uncleanliness that makes your skin crawl. I would get those feelings from time to time when I had a flashback that made me feel as though I were right there reliving it all over again. It's all in the mind, but I can't separate reality from recall. That's the difficulty of Post-Traumatic Stress Disorder (PTSD); you hear things you've heard when they happened, feel things you've felt, and bristle with the same reaction.

My stepdad liked to use objects on me. I am not sure what kind of objects though. I would squeeze my eyes closed and tense up my whole body. The objects were cold and stiff. Sometimes he would just run things over my chest. These are not thoughts that I want to have popping back into my mind, but it happens. When he was done with me, he would leave my room to go shower. All I could think of is him saying, "You're disgusting. I have to go take a shower since I feel so dirty." He raped me but blamed me for what he did. In passing, he would also say things that would make me feel like I was disgusting. Some nights when I would come home, he and my mom would be sitting in the living room and I'd go to the kitchen and as I walked past him, he would say, "Have you taken a shower yet?" I guess that was his plan, to blame me for what's happening and make me feel bad about it so that he didn't have to carry it on his conscience.

My stepfather was very manipulative and persuasive. When you're a teenage girl being raped repeatedly, you begin to believe it is your fault when they tell you that it is and you realize that you haven't fought back. Even if you try to tell yourself that it's not true, you believe somewhere inside of yourself that it is the truth. He would make me feel that I am taking part in it— consenting to it—and made me believe that what he was doing to me was punishment for something I did. I was confused. On one hand, you know the entire action is wrong and that he had done something horrible to you, but then, on the other hand, you're trying to figure out how it was your fault. And then as it continues, you eventually accept it. I began to think it was happening because of my rebellious behavior—cutting myself, drinking alcohol, and every other bad thing that I was doing. He put it into my mind that way and it stuck.

Every time he came into my room, I would freak out and wonder, *Why is he doing this?* I wanted to scream, but I couldn't. I was paralyzed by fear. Then when he was done, the guilt hit. I didn't stop him. I couldn't break this cycle. And though my goal every time was to do something about it, I never could.

The last time, I was 22 years old. In many ways, I encouraged it. I spent the night at my mom's house because I wanted to finally confront him, and I knew he would try to come on to me again. But I felt like I had to stop him. This time had to be different. I had to show him that what he did was wrong, and I could fight back. And then, he did it again. And again, I just lay there—paralyzed. There was nothing I could do. I was upset with myself for putting myself back into that position, and it hurt to think that, even at 22, I was still too weak to confront him, stop him, or to even talk to my mom or anyone else about all that he did and had done to me.

That was one of the biggest defeats in my life and it totally broke me because then I just felt like OK, this really has been my fault, and I'm a loser for thinking otherwise. It just reinforced why I cut, why I drank, why I did drugs, why I didn't come home. It reinforced why I numbed out and had numerous sexual partners when I was very young, which I still can't explain why I did. When you're sexually abused as many times as I was, your self-respect gets lost. My stepdad was a strange and complex man: a neat freak in the house, verbally abusive and controlling toward my mother, sexually aggressive toward me, and kind and friendly to my brother. One thing is certain: He broke me and felt no remorse.

* * *

When I'm triggered, an itchy sensation comes over my body like whole hills of ants are crawling over me. It makes me want to scratch the skin off of my body. I feel the awkward touching again and I want to get rid of it. So, I stand in the shower and let the water run all over me. I've gotten better, but there was a point when I would scrub my skin so hard with a foot pumice stone—the type they use at the nail salon for pedicures—that I would be on the verge of bleeding. I've even shaved the hair off my body because I felt like it's attached to my rapes. It gets real when you're trying to fight the trauma in your mind. It would leave me feeling broken, sore, and mentally a mess for days. Since following Jesus, I've learned a better strategy in the shower now, to turn on worship music to help change my mindset.

Over the years, I've had to rely on medication to manage a lot of the anxiety I feel from this trauma. I'm not ashamed to admit that I use prescription drugs to help me—more survivors should be honest about it or be open to therapy and medication. I saw what the other side looked like as a teenager—drinking, abusing drugs, multiple partners, harming myself—which many people my age still do to drown out the pain. My doctor prescribed Ativan for me, which is extremely addictive, and I had to use that one with care. I've learned that as I grow in Christ and serve others, I have a support system that in turn helps me in my times of need. We all need a support system. Even on medication, the pain can still be overwhelming. There have been times where the post-traumatic stress would hit so hard that I had to see a doctor immediately. Other times, it's back to the shower and occasionally the bathtub. I have had days where I would lay in the bathtub for almost an hour or more. I would draw the water very hot and lie there until my skin would prune. In the shower, I would change the temperature from hot to cold to snap myself out of it. Freezing cold showers bring you back to reality. Sometimes helping yourself when you're feeling lost in your head is all about the tools that you use.

* * *

When I was diagnosed with PTSD in 1999, the past and present met head-on. That was also the year that I began to be more vocal about what had happened with Rolf, but my family refused to believe it, and instead said that I was crazy and should be in a mental hospital to get help. I felt like I had betrayed my mom and that she hated me for it. I chose not to talk to my mom for a long time after she left my house with Rolf that day.

The first couple of days after they left, I slept a lot. My psychiatrist prescribed Valium to me to give my body, mind, and soul a break. I snapped back to life when my dad arrived in California. Yes, there was still one person that cared for and believed me. I can't explain how I really felt about my mom during that time. I was mad, sad, hurt, and broken all at the same time. About nine months after her and her boyfriend left, I met a lady in Monterey, California, while visiting my aunt. She told me that my mom would sit on her balcony at night and cry and that she does believe me. That's when I decided to call her. I remember asking my mom if she believed me, and she said, "Yes, I do." She told me that many times she sits outside at night thinking of me. One week later, she was moved out with one bag and started her life over again (well really, we all started our lives over again). Since then, my mom has been here for me and supports me in any way she can. I am, at this point, praying that she, too, can one day move on from this and hand the feeling of hate for Rolf over to God and replace it with forgiveness.

My family wanted me to press charges, but I was not ready to sit in a courtroom, relive all of that pain again, and then explain to a judge why it took so long for me to speak out and why my family didn't believe me. Though I had documents from every therapist, from the hospital, and from the police station, I didn't want to do it. I felt like my family wanted me to press charges not because of what I went through, but because Rolf had taken my brother's wife away from him. It seemed like they wanted to use me to get back at him. It was such a big slap in the face and I told them I wouldn't do it for that reason. My brother tried to guilt trip me by saying that I had to not think about myself but think about my niece. I reminded him that my niece was his daughter and if he truly believed that I was telling the truth about what happened to me at the hands of my stepfather, who now had access to his young daughter, that he would do anything and everything to get his child away from Rolf. My family continued to make it my responsibility and I felt crappy for not having the ability to press charges. Then to make matters worse, they tried to guilt me by insinuating that if anything happened to my niece, it would be my fault. I encouraged my brother to contact the Child Protective Services and the police, but I am not sure that he ever did.

I recently learned that my niece is now cutting her arms. My family seems to think that I could have prevented that by pressing charges, but my sister-in-law knew about the type of predator she brought into her house. I told them, but no one did anything. While my stepdad and sister-in-law are not together anymore, my niece is still really struggling. She has dropped out of school, cuts herself, smokes weed, and misbehaves. I'm pretty sure I know why. Everybody says she is crazy, just like what they said about me. And now, I'm sure she feels dirty, just as I did.

* * *

"Therefore, if anyone is in Christ, the new creation has come: The old has gone, the new is here!"

2 Corinthians 5:17

Renewal. It's what everybody wants. Throughout the course of our lives, we have done shameful things, and sinful things have been done to us. For those of us who experienced the latter, it can be a hard hurdle to overcome. When our abusers use shame, fear, and doubt to keep us quiet, we're left wondering why it happened and with nowhere to turn. When I think back on my life, I have felt unclean for so long. I felt used, wasted, discarded, unwanted, unprotected, and unloved. I masked all my pain with alcohol, drugs, sex, and every other maladaptive coping strategy you can think of. And in the end, the result was the same: Everything that I did to make myself feel clean only added to the filth. It put me into a deeper hole. That's why these words of Paul are so comforting, whether you're a new believer, old believer, or nonbeliever: "Therefore, if anyone is in Christ, he is a new creation; the old has gone, the new is here."

Here in America, we are obsessed with makeover shows. If you flip to HGTV, you'll see plenty of house flipping, home improvement, and interior redesigning shows than anywhere else on television. It's because we all love a good transformation.

We love seeing old things made new. We love seeing discarded things be revived. It's the same with Jesus; he wants to renovate our hearts and make our minds over. He wants to take all of our filth and make us clean and whole again. It's his job, not ours. No amount of scrubbing, showering, bathing, or any other habits we take on can do for us what the grace of God can. It's a lesson I'm still working into my spirit, but one I want to pass on to you. We don't have to clean ourselves, all we have to do is walk toward Christ, accept him into our lives, and let him do the cleaning. Christ is the perfect renovator for my heart—and he's right for yours, too.

Chapter 7

Just Let Me Die

In October 1991, my fiancé and I had finally moved into our own apartment. I was excited to start nesting and preparing for our life together with our new baby. I was in love with my pregnancy and in my final trimester at the time. The anticipation of giving birth and holding this new baby in my arms for the first time gave me a joy that I had not felt in all my life. Things were finally good for me. I was looking forward to meeting my baby boy.

After we emptied countless boxes, my fiancé and I decided that we needed to go to bed. The next morning, we got up together. He went to work, and I continued working on our still crazy-looking apartment. After an hour or so, I began to feel dizzy and felt all of the energy suddenly drain from my body, which was not unusual for a woman in my condition. I decided to take a quick nap, figuring that a little bit of rest would give me more energy to continue my housework later. What I didn't know then was that this nap would nearly kill me.

As I slept, my asthma—which was already severe—triggered. When I tried to get up, my body was paralyzed and the only thing working was my brain. I became still—and that's the last thing I remembered.

Lucky for me, my fiancé was sent home early from work because of a concussion he got from running into the wall while trying to make his way into the bathroom the night before. We laughed about that for a long time after it happened. That accident saved my life. What neither of us knew at the time was that the gas heater, which was supposed to be warming our new apartment, was releasing deadly carbon monoxide into the air. That's why I was losing consciousness and feeling tired.

When I regained consciousness, it felt like I was still in a dreamlike state. I thought, *Why am I floating where am I?* not knowing whether or not I was fully awake. *What are these doctors doing?* I wondered. I remember yelling at them, begging them to save my baby, but no one was reacting. When I finally became fully conscious, I could see my mom crying, which is weird to me since I had never seen her cry. I was connected to IVs and oxygen. The doctor said that I was gone for a while and that if my fiancé hadn't have grabbed me, carried me down the stairs, and brought me to the hospital—which was two blocks away from our home—the baby and I would have died.

On January 18, 1992, three months after the carbon-monoxide incident, I noticed I wasn't feeling well. We were days away from meeting our new baby and despite being sick, I decided to go to work anyway. I began feeling a sharp pain in my abdomen and, as an expectant mother, I knew that it was time to deliver. I jumped up and down with excitement. I spoke to the doctor and he instructed me to take a bath, wait for the contractions to become eight minutes apart, and then make my way to the hospital.

When we arrived at the hospital, the nurse in charge of my care looked at me nervously. I was 18 years old and a young mother-to-be. When I asked for my doctor, she informed us that he would meet me at a different hospital about 15 miles away. That caused me to feel uneasy and worry, as if something was wrong with my baby or myself. Then the nurse told me that I had to ride in the ambulance without my fiancé. I couldn't understand why.

The blaring sound of the sirens and flashing lights were adding to my concern. When I woke up at the other hospital, an old man was smiling at me. He told me that they were going to be sending him home. My stomach was hurting badly. *Something must have gone wrong*, I thought. I couldn't figure out why I was in the ICU. After trying to analyze what was happening, my family started coming into my room one at a time, including my ex-mother-in-law. I was shocked to see her, since I knew that she didn't care much for me. *I must be in trouble*, I thought. She came in for five minutes and gently kissed my forehead. The doctors ended my visitations and informed my family that I needed rest. Everyone but my mom left the room. She just sat in a chair next to my bed. I asked her to check me because I suddenly felt cold and wondered if I may have peed on myself. I couldn't move much because the cords coming from the monitors and other electronics that were hooked into me restricted my movement. She pushed up the covers above my waist to check on me and abruptly ran out of the room and came back with nurses and doctors. *What's going on?* I wondered.

It was hectic with doctors and nurses, but no one would tell me what was going on. I remember the room spinning and I must have lost consciousness because when I woke up, it was the following day. I asked the attending nurse why a was pastor praying over me. She only answered that the doctor would be in to see me soon.

All I could think was how exciting it was going to be to meet my new baby boy. I knew that I needed to get better soon so I could finally get the chance to hold him. A couple of hours later, the doctor finally made his way to my room with a nurse. She didn't say hello, which I thought was rude. She just handed my doctor some documents, which he proceeded to tell me that I needed to sign. "What am I signing?" I asked. He told me it's to give permission for the autopsy. "Autopsy?" I asked. I voiced my concern to him because I didn't understand why I needed to sign for an autopsy. "Well don't you want to know why your little boy died?" he asked. I felt the room spinning and could not believe what I just heard. All I could think was, *Lord, take me now.* My baby boy, whom I named Dennis, was born alive, but now he was gone—just like that.

* * *

"David noticed that his attendants were whispering among themselves, and he realized the child was dead. 'Is the child dead?' he asked. 'Yes,' they replied, 'he is dead.'"

2 Samuel 12:19

We know the death of David's child was foretold by the prophet Nathan as a decree from God for involvement in committing adultery with Bathsheba, the wife of Uriah the Hittite, one of his mighty men whom he had killed in battle. While those around David knew of his actions and said nothing, God didn't let it slide. As Bathsheba drew near to the end of her pregnancy, God called the child back to him—a heartbreaking blow to David.

Losing what I thought was a healthy pregnancy cut me to my soul. I wanted to isolate myself and do anything but talk openly about my pain. I had to prepare a funeral that I knew I would not be able to attend due to my physical state and the fact that the doctors wouldn't allow me to leave the hospital. I remember going through the funeral home's catalog, which displayed suits and coffins for children, thinking, *This is the last thing you will ever do for your baby.* It was dreamlike, and to this day I daydream about the moment I picked the white coffin with gold handles and a little angel to keep my child company. I didn't go with the traditional suit, but instead I chose a gray and navy Nike sweat suit size 0–3 month. I thought that it would be more comfortable for him.

Signing the release papers from the hospital to the funeral home for my child was still unbelievable to me. Dennis was no longer a part of me. I had never felt as empty and alone in all of my life as I did then. I thought I knew what the worst pain felt like before, but I was wrong. There were numerous complications; my body rejected liters and liters of blood transfusions. The doctors decided the only way to stop me from bleeding out was to perform a complete hysterectomy. My parents came and talked with me about how important it is for me to sign the consent form for the procedure. I thought, *OK, I will just die and be with my child and since I am 18, it is out of my parents' hands and up to me.* Every time I closed my eyes, I could see my baby crawling around the hospital floors looking for me. So, I got ready to die. I did not give my consent for the surgery.

"I will go to him, but he will not return to me."

2 Samuel 12:23

Even though David knew and understood the fate of his choices, it was still difficult to accept. When the joy of birth is replaced by the coldness of death and grief the pain is unimaginable.

The grieving process is different for everyone, but I've learned that allowing yourself time to feel your emotions and understand them is key to healing. You can take the same comfort David did when he learned that his son was stillborn. He proclaimed that though he would not have the joy of seeing his child in this life, he would rejoice in the next when he would "go to him."

Have you ever suffered the loss of a child during pregnancy? Did you allow yourself the time and grace to grieve the death of your baby? If you haven't, I encourage you to do so. Talk to people about how you feel, join a support group, journal, commemorate your child, or do anything that makes you feel you have done something. Healing will take time.

The Bible says, "The Lord is close to the brokenhearted and saves those who are crushed in spirit." Press into God deeply. He is the restorer of all things and He upholds the faithful. In the book of Job, we learn that Job had seven sons and three daughters and, under testing, lost them all. When he wrestles with his faith in God and finally comes to terms with the Lord's sovereignty in his life, the Bible says, "After Job had prayed for his friends, the Lord restored his fortunes and gave him twice as much as he had before. All his brothers and sisters and everyone who had known him before came and ate with him in his house. They comforted and consoled him over all the trouble the Lord had brought on him, and each one gave him a piece of silver and a gold ring. The Lord blessed the latter part of Job's life more than the former part. He had fourteen thousand sheep, six thousand camels, a thousand yoke of oxen, and a thousand donkeys. And he also had seven sons and three daughters."

It's been over 25 years since my loss. God has since blessed me with six children in a beautiful blended family. I am married to my wonderful husband of 12 years and, through our union and my husband's faith, I found everlasting love in the arms of God. When our losses seem great we must remember that our God is greater.

Chapter 8

The Apple Doesn't Fall Far

My mom has always had to be a strong woman, but that's probably because of the way she was brought up. She wasn't allowed to go to school, but instead she had to raise her siblings when my grandparents went to work. I think this is why she had such a tough exterior—nothing could get to her. I also think she was always in a lot more pain than anyone else could see.

When it was my mom, my brother, and I, we were always good. We had good times. She always worked a lot, but when she was home, she'd cook, and we'd listen to a lot of music and hang out. We'd go shopping and then go out to dinner. She loved lying on the couch watching TV with us or playing some word games. She was the perfect mom. I remember going on vacations together and we would enjoy our time. One of my favorite memories was when we went on a vacation to Morocco and had a blast. It was just the two of us, and we stayed at nice hotels and went dancing.

When she met her boyfriend, Rolf, that all changed. Though they never married, he lived with us; they were together for 17 years.

She started going out more and went from casual dresses to miniskirts and high heels. I think the reason for that was because he was much younger than her. It always felt like when my mom had a significant other, everything was about him and how he made her happy at that time. It seemed like my brother and I were in the way of things all the time. When things were going well in her relationships, we were an afterthought but when they fought, we were good enough for her again.

Sometimes she would abandon us while she was off being happy in her relationship. Once when I was about 13 years old, she stayed for what seemed like forever at Rolf's house with him and his mom. My 15-year-old brother and I were left home alone. She would stop by every once in a while, to check in on us. It was scary for me because, in the back of my mind, I felt as though she might walk out on us completely at any second.

This was my mom's pattern. She found her security in men. I don't know if that was because she never had a childhood of her own or felt loved as a child. And maybe that's why she always preferred being around younger men. I suppose it made her feel like she was reliving her teen years. That's the only way it made sense to me. All I know is throughout my whole life, I only remember my mom being by herself maybe for two years. She always had long relationships and it didn't matter how her boyfriends would treat her, she would stay with them. I watched my mom work hard—she owned restaurants—and then fund everything for her boyfriend. If he wanted a new motorcycle, she bought it; a new Mercedes, no problem; the best furniture and entertainment, of course. Then I would watch as he called her names in public. He would tell her that she was old, and he and his friends would laugh. I didn't understand why he mattered so much to her. I know he was young—and to her very handsome—and a lot of younger women wanted him. Maybe it was it; she had someone that everyone else wanted.

The irony is this: As much as I didn't like my mom's relationship patterns, I repeated many of them unknowingly. While I have always been more protective of my kids than she was of my brother and me, I let other things slide, like abuse, much like she did. It seems that you can sometimes become the very thing you try to avoid.

My First Husband

My first husband and I started dating in June 1989 and got married in February 1993. I had just turned 19. It only took three short months before things turned bad. At that time in Germany, young men were still drafted into the military and they could be called upon at any time once they turned 18. He was 22 when his letter arrived in the mail. We already had a child on the way and he knew that if we were to get married he wouldn't have to go. So, when the letter arrived for him to join the military, he came home and said that we were going to have to get married now. I agreed, even though we had a lot to work on to make our relationship work.

When I was five months pregnant with my first son, my husband had a soccer tournament. I used to attend all of his games, but that day I wasn't feeling well. My asthma was bothering me, so I decided to stay at home. He assured me he would be home as soon as possible to take me to the ER. We were living at his mom's house at the time and she ended up having to take me to the doctor. They ended up giving me some breathing treatments. When we got home, he was there and had been drinking already. I told him about my afternoon and how I ended up in the ER. He laughed. I started yelling at him and then we argued. That's when the unthinkable happened— he slapped me and threw me across the room. That was the first time he had ever laid his hands on me. He immediately started crying and became apologetic. Since he was drinking, I accepted his apology. In hindsight, I totally let him get away with it and it wasn't the right thing to do because he eventually hit me a second time.

Sometime after our son died, we had an incident where he got really angry with me. I decided to go to a friend's house for a few days. It was Father's Day and the doorbell rang. When I opened the door, he walked in and he started hitting me. I was caught completely off guard not knowing what was happening. He kept yelling something about me seeing some other guy. I only felt the first couple of punches and kicks. He hit me so hard that he blacked my eye, split my lip, and caused me to need serious dental work. One of my friends took me to the hospital where I ended up staying the night. After two weeks, I went back to him of course. His charm and humor had me convinced that things would be different this time. He continued to be physically abusive. It only got better when I got pregnant with our daughter, Denise. He had angry outbursts, but he didn't hit me. He would blow up and then he would leave sometimes for a couple hours and sometimes for days. After Denise was born, I had finally had enough of him and kicked him out of our house and our lives when the police came to our house and turned our house upside down searching for drugs. There was no coming back from that; I had a child to protect and no heartache in the world would change that.

I always thought Denise could save his life. After being away from him for a while, I learned he was on heroin and not doing well at all. When Denise was 2 years old, she and I visited him at the clinic during Christmas to bring him things that he needed. I met with his doctor and his therapist since every time he ran away from his treatment center, he'd come to my house. I would feel sorry for him and let him in. He began to steal from me and then one day he locked himself in my bathroom for three hours. I had to ask a neighbor to come to my house and kick in the door. We found him lying on the floor, blood everywhere, with a needle still in his arm. I called 911. Not long after that, I met with his doctor and therapist who advised me not to take him into my home ever again. His therapist said that I was enabling him, and he was down to two choices now, either the drugs would kill him, or he was going to recover. There was nothing more I could do for him.

This is when I realized that Denise and I had to get away from this situation so that she would have no memory of it. We parted ways in June of 1993. That October I met the man who would become my second husband.

My Second Husband

My second husband was an SP (Security Police Officer) in the Air Force. When we first met, he seemed like a dream come true. Little did I know I was entering another nightmare. I saw all the signs but convinced myself it would be all better once we left Germany. This was my ticket to start over and heal from the pain of my first marriage—a means of getting away from everything and everybody in Germany that I wanted to disassociate with or forget altogether.

I soon learned that he was a control freak. He was absolutely possessive, controlling, and manipulative. When he was around my parents, he had such a nice-guy persona that they thought he could never do anything wrong. But he was mentally abusive toward me. My dad saw this firsthand once when he came to visit us for three weeks. While with us, he saw a side of my husband that he had not seen before, and it shocked him.

You would think that after all I had endured in Germany with my first husband's physical and verbal abuse that I wouldn't tolerate it again, but I did. The manipulative side of my second husband was better than having to deal with my first husband's drug use, and my mom still being with her boyfriend. I was just happy to be on the other side of the world despite the abuse. They are all in Germany; I was in the United States. As long as I could protect Denise, who was 4 years old at the time, I felt like we were going to be OK. In March of 1998, we had our son, Denell. I was ecstatic.

The mental abuse eventually gave way to physical outbursts. Not hitting me but displaying his anger outside of himself. I finally had enough when one day, I confronted him about exchanging pictures of me with some guys on the internet. He became so enraged that he punched a hole in the wall and threw his computer monitor across the living room. Denise was sitting in the corner and she started crying when she saw it. When I looked over at my baby crying, that was the end of it for me. While I patterned a lot of tolerance of abuse from seeing my mother's relationships, I remembered the sting of feeling unprotected from the men in her life. I always said that when I had kids, they would know that I am here for them no matter what is happening and no matter where we are. So, while I endured abuse, I protected my children from it and that caused me to leave him after his last outburst. He threatened to kill himself, something he commonly did when he felt the need to regain control. It happened every time I tried to leave him. He would say that if he killed himself, it was going to be my fault. The day I finally left him, he was sitting in the garage with a gun to his head. I just told him to do the world and himself a favor and pull the trigger—and then I got into our car with the kids, drove off, and never looked back. As we headed down the street, I was praying that we would not hear that gunshot and we didn't. He was manipulative until the end of our relationship.

I decided to stay in California even though we weren't together anymore. I went to Germany for a little while, but I came back. I took care of my kids, went to school, and worked. I did everything I could to make a life for us and that's when I realized that the man that was my friend for the longest time would be the man to become my current husband, who I'll tell you about next.

* * *

I think that I messed up a lot because of the things I saw growing up. So much of what I became, accepted, and tolerated in my life stems from the relationship that I had with my mom. I'm not putting my choices on her, but unless we recognize the patterns we unconsciously develop and make purposeful changes, we become products of our environment. I saw men abuse my mother with no consequence. I watched my mom try to kill herself. I think I was around maybe 8 or 9 years old and, in that same year, my dad tried to kill himself. I didn't grow up easy and I didn't always feel loved. I don't think I've ever once heard my mom tell me, "I love you," but that's all I wanted for her to do. Hug me and say, "I love you."

As a child and even as a teenager, I did not feel protected by my mother. I learned to not value myself through this. I didn't protect myself from men who were physically violent, verbally abusive, or just plain mean toward me. I allowed anything to go. I got to the point where I didn't care if the people came or went. I expected it because it was what was modeled for me. We never know as kids how things will affect us as adults.

I wonder if you're like me? Staying in bad relationships when you know the danger of them—danger to you, to your children, and toxic for all. When we don't speak up, what are we showing our children? We have to think about what is it they are seeing, what it is that they are processing, and how they're going to use that information when they grow up. I wanted to stop the cycle. I want you to stop your cycle, too.

When my dad tried to commit suicide, I found him. It's something my dad would never talk about again. With my mom's attempt, I've talked about it since then and she said it wasn't intentional, but I know it was intentional. My brother and I had to call 911. When they came they had to rid her body of all the pills she took and she had to stay in a psychiatric ward for a couple of weeks, which was terrible. Even to this day, she will deny that it ever happened and that makes me feel angry because I was right there—I remember. These are just a few of the things that further complicated my relationship with my mom.

I love my Mom and I'd do anything for her, but I don't expect anything from her. What I have learned from the tough and pain-filled relationship with my mom was that I wanted to care for and protect my kids better. I never wanted them to feel the same way that I did. The downside is that it has made me a more overprotective mother, which is not necessarily a good thing.

My dad messed up a lot, but even still, he's always been my hero. Our relationship is weird like that. He's always had a drinking issue, but he was always working and always providing for my brother and me. He even did the simple things well, like making sure we got to our doctor's appointments. He told me that he was sorry he couldn't be there in my most difficult times when he should have been. Sometimes when we were with him, he would be so drunk that he needed to sleep in the car before driving us back to our mother's house. My brother and I would sit in the car for a couple of hours waiting for dad to sober up. Sometimes when that happened, we just got out the car and walked the four miles home, even if it was in the middle of the night. Despite it all, I felt secure with my dad. I always knew with him that if there would be nobody here in the world to help me when I needed someone, I could call him, and he would be on the next plane out. And that's probably because he doesn't try to defend himself from the hurts he committed in the past. He's never made me feel like it was all in my mind. When he came to visit me in California, we sat and talked about everything. He listened to me and he apologized. He said, "Look, I wanted to be here, but I just wasn't ready to do that." I accepted, and we moved on. And that's all I've ever wanted from my mom.

* * *

"Follow my example, as I follow the example of Christ."

1 Corinthians 11:1

Throughout the entire recorded human history in Scripture, men followed examples that did not work for them. Despite God giving Adam and Eve a perfect example, our hearts have always done what we wanted them to do. And it's not that man cannot create a good example to follow but is that men are flawed, and Scriptures tell us that our eyes are to be on Christ and to follow his example.

When I look back over my life and see the things my mom has done, the way that she lived her life, and how even as much as I did not want to become like her, subconsciously I did. The things I saw in her that I didn't want for me eventually found their way into my life. I unknowingly carried around her pain, her fears, her insecurities, her tolerance for abuse, and her lack of self-esteem. I did what was modeled for me. The only example I had was her life and it's amazing how that happens in life. Now, as a Christian, I have the example of Jesus Christ. I have the example of many righteous men and women in Scripture that have gone before me. I have the example of people around me who also strive to walk in Christ—good, godly examples.

As the Scripture says, we have been put on this earth to be imitators of Christ, and not each other or other people. Think about your life. Think about the people you admire, the people that you model your life after, or even the people you don't wish to be like. Did you become like any of them? Chances are you did.

In 1 Peter 2:21, Peter says, "To this you were called, because Christ suffered for you, leaving you an example that you should follow in his steps." That is what God wants for us, for us to follow the footsteps of Christ. In His example, from His life came the fruits of the spirit which are: love, joy, peace, patience, kindness, goodness, faithfulness, gentleness, and self-control of all. Many things I didn't grow up with or know of at the time. But I can't go around for the rest of my life blaming my outcomes on my mother. Now that I have learned about forgiveness and the grace of God, I can look back and understand her choices and how they affected me, and I can now make better choices and be a better example for my own children. Maybe that's something you'll want to consider, too. That's how repentance works. We learn, forgive, turn away, and live better. As the poet Maya Angelou says, "Do the best you can until you know better. Then when you know better, do better." That's the example of Christ made alive.

Chapter 9

Godsent

Lawrence and I started off as good friends. I would watch his kids and he would watch mine. About three or four months after my second husband moved out, we got together. The funny thing is I used to tell Lawrence that if he were the last man on earth, I would never date him. I remember the days that he would call me and ask me if I could hang out with one of his "friends" while he was getting rid of the one that's on his couch. I still chuckle about the time when his "friends" came to celebrate Denise and Denell's birthday. His ex-wife was there with his oldest son and so was his girlfriend with his 5-month-old daughter, oh and the ex-girlfriend that was pregnant with his child came, too. I loved Lawrence for who he was as my friend, but never thought that he would be the one God sent for me.

Lawrence proved to be a different kind of man though. With my second husband, it was about me escaping another bad relationship, which led to us getting together and eventually marrying, but with Lawrence, we had a real friendship. He would tell me everything and we felt comfortable around one another.

I approached this relationship differently than I had in the past. Lawrence and I decided to have an open relationship for the first three years because I wasn't ready to have another man telling me what to do, how to live, or where to be. I didn't want to have to answer to anyone yet. I was over the pain from my last marriage, and yes, he enjoyed having someone to experience life with while still being who he wanted to be. Things were working out well for Lawrence and me until he got ordered by the Air Force to go to the Netherlands. I decided to go back to Germany ahead of him, but before he got to the Netherlands, he invited me to come there to live with him when he arrived. He told me he was ready for a real relationship and that we needed to end our open relationship. He wanted to settle down together and look for a house, so that's what we did. While we looked for a house in the Netherlands, within six weeks, he was ordered to go to Germany.

Living together was good the first year. I was far enough away from my family to drive to see them, but I had enough distance to know that they wouldn't be knocking on my door unexpectedly. Our house was perfect, and our life was good, but I suppose that after living in Germany again for three years, I was bound to get caught up in all of the feelings and emotions from my traumatic past. While dealing with it all was hard, Lawrence stuck by me.

It didn't take long for old patterns to resurface. Since I had lost any trust that I had in people, particularly men, I still functioned like we had an open relationship. I didn't care what he did. That led Lawrence to have a couple of affairs, but it didn't break us really because I had no expectations from the relationship and I expected that he would cheat anyway. There were a couple of times where I suspected that he was having affairs and even though in those times it wasn't true, I still didn't care. I let him do whatever he wanted to, which always caused issues between us because he felt like I didn't really care about him based on my attitude.

Outside of our relationship, I stayed far enough away from family and friends. It wasn't until one morning when we were supposed to go to the zoo with the kids that something felt off. My hip and hands started hurting and burning. I couldn't move my legs because my hip was hurting so badly. Despite going to the doctor, the pain went on for a couple of weeks. I had several appointments and had my blood drawn. When I met with the doctor again, he told me it was all psychologically related and then recommended I go to therapy. I should have known living in Germany again would trigger something in me, but my life was going so well, so I didn't see it coming.

It got to a point where I couldn't get out of bed and I didn't eat or sleep. The doctors put me on meds, which did not help at all since I couldn't function on them enough to take care of my kids. My therapist said these things were happening because I never talked about my trauma to anyone, nor did I let anyone see my emotions. That's when I decided to go to an inpatient clinic.

Having to see therapists and be admitted to a clinic was rough for Lawrence and the kids. It was supposed to be for six weeks, but my stay got extended to nine weeks. I was allowed to go home on weekends but when I got home, I felt so lost in my own house that I wanted to go back to the clinic. I liked it better there at that point in time because I was able to cry when I wanted to and scream without judgment. I wasn't supposed to have or make phone calls while there, but I didn't care though. I always tried to call the kids and when I did, I could hear Lawrence fighting with them in the background. It was stressful because there was nothing I could do. My mom was also there helping Lawrence take care of the kids. When I finally came home, things sorted themselves out and got back to normal. My doctor prescribed different meds, which made me feel much better, but it took me a while to get back to my daily routine. Everything I learned at the clinic I used to the best of my ability at home. After a while though, life has a way of catching up with you again and you feel as though you've gained nothing.

We eventually moved to Norway, which went pretty decent. Everything was going well until the day my daughter was touched inappropriately by a family member. That brought the monster out of me. All of the trauma and emotion from my past came roaring back to the surface. The emotions I felt that day could never compare to any pain I have ever felt before. Growing up the way I did, my sole purpose in life was and still is to protect my children. I wanted to just hold my child and run as far away as I could, which was not possible because my daughter ran away the week prior to us finding out what had happened. The thought of my baby sharing my nightmares was an unbearable thought. What if she turned to drugs? What if she felt so alone and helpless that she tried to commit suicide?

That day, I was again in this dreamlike state when you scream loudly but no one can hear you.

After talking to my dad whom my daughter spoke to about the incident and talking to the family member, it came out that what he had done was considered a form of sexual assault. When I learned that, I wanted him arrested and locked up, but my daughter said she didn't want that. That year was a really tough one, six months after my child left for Germany, my ex-husband, her father, lost his battle against drugs and was found dead after overdosing. My daughter's dad was clean and free of all drugs and alcohol for eight years. He was available to his child and we became the friends we were supposed to be; he was coaching little league soccer and working as a foreman for an industrial mechanic. He would come and stay at our house to watch the kids so that Lawrence and I could go on dates or sometimes away for the weekend. The only consolation we really had was that the minister that spoke at his funeral told us that just a few weeks prior to him overdosing that he was seeking God at a local church where he lived.

After four years in Norway, our next orders were to Virginia, which was brand new for us. With his brother now close by, Lawrence invited him and his wife to come and bless the house because he was a pastor. Within the first two weeks of moving in, his brother told us that we could have no alcohol in the house, which I thought was absolutely crazy. It was my house and he was telling us what we couldn't have in it. I shrugged it off and agreed, choosing instead to just hide my alcohol inside of my car. Once he left, I brought it all back inside the house. Lawrence had my back though. No matter what the situation was, he always said, "Look, we're married, and we are one." I never felt that way with anyone before, so I didn't always appreciate it. I would just think, *Yeah, whatever.* Honestly, half of the time I didn't even feel married. It's hard to get that close to someone when you don't trust them or anyone, no matter what they do or say.

Despite it all though, Lawrence was always different. I believe for the last five years—I know for sure for the last three years—he has been on his knees in the morning and at night praying for me. I guess that's why we've made it through a lot of difficult times. He never lost faith in us.

* * *

When it came to the sexual abuse that I had to endure in my past and the reactions that I had to it, up until recently, Lawrence just didn't know everything about it. He knew some things about my past before we started dating, but not much. No one did. He had no idea because I never told him. There were times in the marriage when I wanted to tell him, but I couldn't get it out, or, when I did, he couldn't process it. Whenever I did try to talk to him in those vulnerable moments I was ready to talk, he would say not to think like, "Don't think about it" or "Get over it." Then he would ask why was I thinking about that kind of stuff. I finally gave up; there was no talking to him about it because he may never understand. He didn't know the depths of my hurts and it was hard for me to share them. It wasn't that he was insensitive to my pain. He was just not informed. Now, when the subject comes up and I want to talk about it, he is able to listen and understand. He asks me if I need space. It's good that he has made this much progress, but there is still more to tell—a lot of details—and it will take time because I feel like he's not ready for that much at one time. A lot of people are not ready for my story. When you're a rape and abuse survivor in a marriage where your partner doesn't know your whole history, your first instinct is to try to protect them. It's not that you want to keep secrets; it's just emotionally charged and heavy. That's not an easy burden for husbands to bear without proper help and guidance.

Lawrence always did treat me with respect, something I wasn't always grateful for, but I am now. He just accepted me as I was and that was really hard for me. No one had ever done that. It wasn't until I became a Christian that I really felt married (and that was after 10 years). It's hard to explain, but I look at him now and think, *Wow, I'm really married to this man.* As he began to understand more, it became really hard because the more you talk about the abuse you've had to live with, the more you'll have to face bad days and I didn't want him to see me looking like a wreck. I especially didn't want the kids to see me that way, so, for the most part, I just tried to be so strong, but at the same time I felt like I was about to explode. There were times when I would lock myself in the bathroom and sit there for a couple hours to try to deal with the pain as best I could.

Prior to knowing God, the only time I ever felt good in the last few years was when I was really drunk. It felt great when I was drinking, but it didn't feel good the next day because I felt like I shouldn't have been out there in the first place. Lawrence just loved me through it. He stayed home and took care of the kids while I was out drinking. Sometimes I wouldn't even come home until 7 o'clock in the morning. It was hard on him, but he was still there for me. When you're trying to manage pain on your own, that's your normal. That's just what you do. It doesn't matter how many therapists will tell you that this could be done differently; if you don't know how to change it, you can't. You just keep doing the same things over and over again. It's a trap—and it hurts the people you love.

Lawrence and I have been together for almost 18 years now and it's taken me nearly all of those years to let my guard down. But he stood by my side, never abused me, prayed for me, and loved my kids, and me, and he did his best to show me Jesus. He was truly a godsend to me.

* * *

"As it is written in Isaiah the prophet: I will send my messenger ahead of you, who will prepare your way—a voice of one calling in the wilderness, 'Prepare the way for the Lord, make straight paths for him.' And so John the Baptist appeared in the wilderness, preaching a baptism of repentance for the forgiveness of sins."

Mark 1:2-4

The people of Israel got a real treat when they saw John the Baptist in the desert. It had been a few hundred years since a prophet has brought a message from God to the people. John came preparing hearts for Jesus. He wasn't the Christ, as some thought he might be, just the one pointing the way.

Lawrence was a John for me. When I met him, I was lost. There was silence in my spiritual life. I chose to live for myself and view the world through a cracked and broken lens. Yet here was this man who loved me, cared for me, prayed for me, and took our children to church faithfully. He was my rock. His light eventually pointed me toward the love of Jesus when God began to stir within my heart. I thank God every day for that.

I think we all have a John somewhere in our lives. Some person who has been loving us and praying for us, and listening to our heartaches and sadness, yet not afraid to stay there with us when the going gets tough. Who is your John? Who is trying to point you to Jesus, or point you back to him if your faith is feeling weak? If you know who that person is, get together with them and open up about your need for a closer walk with God. If you don't know, keep your eyes and your heart open. When you hear it, their voice will be unmistakable

Chapter 10

Don't Send Me to Hell

Growing up, I never believed in God. I believed that He existed, but I didn't worship Him, pray to Him, or put my faith in Him. I came from a family that didn't go to church. My great grandma was the most religious person that I saw. She taught me how to pray, even though it would be decades before I applied those lessons. Every morning and night she would be on her knees. Watching her was the extent of my church and religious experience.

That's what makes my marriage to Lawrence unique. Though I lived like I chose to, he was a faithful man. He grew up in the Methodist church on his home island of Antigua, which is in the Caribbean Sea between Puerto Rico and Trinidad and Tobago. He would walk for miles to attend church as a kid. Even after we were married, I still didn't attend church. Lawrence would dress the kids and take them. I remember how much me not going would upset my daughter, Denise. She wanted me to go to church so that I would be able to go to heaven with the rest of the family.

When we moved from Norway to Virginia, something began to stir inside of me. Every day I drove to work, I would see this black and yellow sign for Upward Church. The more I passed it, the more I felt like the sign was telling me that I needed to come in. One evening when I got home from work, I said to Lawrence, "You know, we need to go to that church." And he looked at me and said, "What? You want to go to church?" He started laughing and asked what was going on with me. I repeated to him that I just had a feeling that I needed to go to this particular church. I couldn't explain it, but I felt oddly drawn to it and I wanted to be there.

We got all dressed up the following Sunday and went to Upward Church. Lawrence was wearing slacks, a button-down shirt, and a tie. I can't remember what I was wearing, but I was cleaned up that day. Our girls were wearing dresses. The church greeters were dressed in jeans and T-shirts at the door and inside the lobby, there was coffee and pastries. When we got inside the sanctuary, we saw the pastor wearing jeans and flip-flops!—a complete shock to both of us. It was a different experience than either of us were used to. The music was contemporary concert-style worship in the dark and there were no windows. Smoke was billowing from the stage while the band played. Lawrence looked at me and said, "Wow, this is a weird place." At that time, my son said, "I don't think Uncle Jerry's going to like this. This is not a church." Jerry is a pastor and Lawrence's brother.

We stayed around after service to meet some of the people at the church. It felt awkward. The people were welcoming and nice, but it felt too nice. We thought, "What's really going on here. Was it a cult type of thing that would suck us in and there was no way out?" We weren't sure if we would ever return, but when next Sunday came, I said to Lawrence, "OK, I want to go to Upward Church again." So that's when we started going regularly.

I'd like to say that's when my life changed, but it didn't. I was still drinking and doing my own thing on Saturday night and on Sundays I would walk into the church and I'd just feel different (yes, I was one of those types!). Despite my uneven lifestyle of partying and church, something was beginning to change within me even though the rest of my life didn't reflect it. Shamefully, I still came to service at 10 a.m. hungover after getting home at 5 a.m. from a night of drinking. But the more we went to church, the more I felt comfortable there and it was a good feeling.

It didn't take long before I began to notice that whenever it was time for church, I started having panic attacks. I told Lawrence that I didn't want to go back anymore, but he insisted that we continue to go to church as a family, and eventually we started going to Refuel on Wednesday nights.

I felt like I was having a nervous breakdown the first time I went to Refuel. It was overwhelming despite it being a service devoted to prayer and worship. During the service, I began to cry and was unable to stop, so Lawrence took me home and I told him that I didn't think I could go anymore. He explained to me that the closer I got to God, the more the Enemy would intervene to try and disrupt any chance of a relationship. That made sense, and, when Sunday came again, I went back to church. Even though I didn't want to go, something inside of me told me I needed to be in this church.

We continued going to Upward Church and then one Sunday, Pastor Craig Walker, the lead pastor, preached a message about sexual predators. It made me think. Throughout my life, I made excuses for my mom's boyfriend; that he was mentally ill, or that there was something else wrong with him and that's why he did it. But as I listened to Pastor Craig speak, he was telling us that those behaviors are not okay. He said that they were not sick people and that they had no excuses; that people who commit these acts do them because they want to do them and because they can do them. When I heard that, I didn't know how to take it. I was holding on to the hope that they were just sick men and that they didn't willfully choose to rape me. Coming to that understanding changed everything for me right then and there and, internally, things got bad for me. That closeness I began to feel with God felt shaky. I began to feel unsure about what I had just heard and about being in church as I sat there stunned.

After that sermon, it was really hard for me to go back to church. I was having mixed emotions and it felt like I was having a nervous breakdown. So many thoughts were going through my head. The way I understood it was that I was choosing to hold on to the past and remain a victim of my circumstances—that, somehow, I had asked for all of these things to happen to me. But I knew I didn't choose to be a victim. I felt conflicted and, because of where my mind was, Pastor Craig's words hurt me. It was more than I could handle.

Lawrence recommended that I talk to somebody, someone other than a therapist this time. I agreed. I can't tell you how many therapists I had seen at that point. My therapists taught me how to keep my head above water, but they never taught me how to swim. I learned how to manage, but there was no post-traumatic growth happening within me. So, I grabbed my phone and called Pastor David, the family pastor at Upward Church. I asked him if we could talk. He agreed to meet with me, and he invited Pastor Craig to be there as well.

* * *

We met at Upward on a Wednesday night at 8:30 p.m. after our midweek Refuel service. Lawrence and I were sitting on the couch in Pastor Craig's office. Pastor Craig and Pastor David pulled up a couple of chairs. I told Pastor Craig how I felt as I listened to his sermon on sexual abuse and victimhood. He asked whether or not I wanted to talk about it further. In a shorter version, I shared my whole story with him and then they prayed for me on the spot. As I sat there in the pastor's office cursing and venting years of bottled up anger, pain, and frustration, I noticed that he didn't seem to mind. He just listened and let me speak my mind. I told him that I was sorry, but he encouraged me to let it all out and said that I had to get rid of it. Through the grace they showed me, I learned that day that it was okay for me to be upset about the things that had happened to me.

I finally got it all out of my system. Pastor Craig then shifted gears and began to talk to me about forgiveness and learning how to forgive the people who had hurt me. Though hearing that bothered me, he highlighted the fact that it was not about me and I could be mad or upset all I wanted to be, but I still had to make the choice to forgive. He said that if I couldn't, I had to give it to God. I felt angry at their teaching to forgive everything; let it all go. They reminded me that there was no excuse for what was done to me, but that telling myself that they had some kind of mental issue was an excuse—my mind finding a way to justify it and by default protect my abusers. As I sat there trying to stay composed, I thought, *How am I supposed to not hate them more than I did before after hearing this? How was I going to ever forgive those people?* I sat there on the couch confused and angry. I could not get it into my brain that if I didn't forgive the sins of others, God wouldn't forgive my sins. Lawrence started massaging my shoulders in an effort to help me calm down. For the first time, he didn't give me an, "It's going to be okay" response. I felt like he had my back, but he was allowing the words to sink in even though he knew that I wasn't okay.

I felt like God was punishing me. I couldn't just forgive these men for the wrong they did to me. I didn't know *how* to forgive them. The pain they caused me had followed me throughout my entire life. Pastor David reiterated it was Biblical to forgive, and I said, "So you're telling me that I'm going to hell because I cannot forgive them for what they have done to me! Do you understand that what they did to me has ruined my life?" His position did not change. I was hurt and had a lot of things to think about that night and over the course of the next few days. I realized it was good for Lawrence to have heard me open up fully about the rapes and abuses that I had endured as a teenager. He knew things had happened to me, but for the first time, he really understood the depth of it and I felt he would be able to support me in a different way now.

After calming down, I felt better and had a positive outlook on the situation when I left Pastor Craig's office. Lawrence, who was happy that I reached out to Pastor David, was excited that we chose to give God a chance to work through my healing. As I went home, I thought about what Pastors Craig and David had said and wondered how I was going to forgive my rapist. That's when I started thinking about all of the bad things that I had done in my life and thought, *Well, we all want forgiveness.* It was Pastor Craig who said to me in our meeting, "All day long, this is what you're going to tell yourself, 'I choose to forgive.'" That thinking helped me a lot and I told myself all day long the next day and each day after that that I would choose to forgive. Every time something crazy came to my mind, I would stop the thought and say, "I choose to forgive," even though it was really hard for me.

I started praying every day, asking God to help me forgive. After a few months, I was able to say that I had forgiven them. On Wednesdays at Refuel, I felt inspired to pray about it with the church and I would put my rapist on the prayer board and ask people to pray for him. I was shocked at how my heart had softened and went from hating him to hoping that he had straightened his life and he would meet and walk with God. I even started to have a mental shift and thought of the good things he did and the good memories he gave our family. That's when I knew I had finally forgiven him. As I was singing and worshipping, I could feel my heart being touched. For a woman who had only known heartache, abandonment, abuse, and pain,

I suddenly felt free for the first time. I knew that it came from extending that first act of forgiveness and it is a feeling that I never wanted to lose again.

* * *

"This is what you are to say to Joseph: 'I ask you to forgive your brothers the sins and the wrongs they committed in treating you so badly.' Now please forgive the sins of the servants of the God of your father. When their message came to him, Joseph wept."

Genesis 50:17

There is nothing more betraying than the sting of being hurt and abused by the people closest to you; those in your own home who are supposed to love and protect you. Maybe you know the story of Joseph and maybe you don't. As a 17-year-old boy, God gave Joseph dreams. Convinced to not allow his dreams to come to pass—both of his dreams involved him ruling over his mother, father, and 10 brothers—his brothers hatched a plan to have him killed and thus end his dreaming. God, however, had another plan. Instead of killing Joseph as they had planned, Reuben convinced his brothers to instead place him in a well. You get the feeling that Reuben began to feel remorseful and guilty about what they were going to do to Joseph and made this suggestion to buy himself a little time to rescue his little brother. No one knows for certain, but when Reuben went away, the other nine brothers saw a caravan of traveling Midianites and sold Joseph to them. The Midianites eventually sold Joseph into slavery in Egypt.

While in Egypt, Joseph's character and work ethic enabled him to become the top servant of Potiphar, the captain of Pharaoh's guards. Undoubtedly, he made the most of a bad situation until his young and handsome features captured the attention of his master's wife. When he refused to sin against God by sleeping with her, she had him jailed on false rape charges.

Pain compounds when there is no encouragement to be found. When there is no relief in sight, we can become discouraged and lose hope. I did for many years. Joseph was young and innocent, much like I was, and was forced to grow up quickly and under unwanted conditions. I get that, too. But even in despair, we know that God is at work. He was with Joseph when he went from servant to prisoner.

Joseph rose through the ranks in prison because of his faith and his character. He made the most of a bad situation with God by his side. Then an opportunity arose when the chief baker and cupbearer of Pharaoh displeased the king and were placed in prison. While there, one night they each had a dream that required interpretation. Joseph, who was given the gift of dream interpretation from God, told both men what their dreams meant (though one was unfavorable!) and asked only in return that they help him gain an audience with Pharaoh, so he could try to appeal his imprisonment. They promised. When the day came for both men to go before Pharaoh, the chief baker was executed as Joseph predicted, but the cupbearer was restored. Unfortunately, perhaps in his relief, he forgot about Joseph.

At this point, you could imagine how all of the years of compounded hurts, lies, and broken promises had affected him. Joseph, a man who as a boy dreamed that he would be a ruler, was a slave and regarded as a criminal. I wonder if he asked God: "Why did you give me those dreams if I'm rotting in a prison?"; "Why did you get my hopes up only to pull the rug out from under me again and again?"; "Don't you care?" I only wonder because that's how it feels when every time you think you're getting your life sorted out, you fall down again.

Eventually, Joseph is released when he is able to interpret Pharaoh's dreams. He was made second in command after Pharaoh, but it's interesting that despite his now-good position, he still had some unresolved bitterness. For some of us who endure sexual abuse, we can hide the hurt behind accomplishments— advanced degrees, promotions, good lives. The downside: Success doesn't remove our pain; it just masks it until the next hurt arrives or the wounds are reopened or triggered. You need only to look at the names of Joseph's kids to figure that out:

> "Before the years of famine came, two sons were born to Joseph by Asenath daughter of Potiphera, priest of On. Joseph named his firstborn Manasseh and said, 'It is because God has made me forget all my trouble and all my father's household.' The second son he named Ephraim and said, 'It is because God has made me fruitful in the land of my suffering.'"

Genesis 41:50-52

Joseph's thoughts were to forever forget his troubles and his family and he referred to Egypt as the land of his suffering.

When a famine strikes the land, Joseph's brothers come to get grain and failed to recognize him. He tested their hearts, and in time, he revealed himself to them. A tearful family reunion. In his final words to his son from his deathbed, Jacob asks Joseph to forgive his brothers for the sin they committed against him:

> *"When Joseph's brothers saw that their father was dead, they said, 'What if Joseph holds a grudge against us and pays us back for all the wrongs we did to him?' So they sent word to Joseph, saying, 'Your father left these instructions before he died: 'This is what you are to say to Joseph: I ask you to forgive your brothers for the sins and the wrongs they committed in treating you so badly.' Now please forgive the sins of the servants of the God of your father.' When their message came to him, Joseph wept."*

Genesis 50:15-17

* * *

Forgiveness is hard, but it must be done. As I sat in my pastor's office, I was challenged to find a way to forgive some awful, deeply personal offenses that changed my life and robbed me of my innocence. I learned that forgiveness isn't about my rapist or letting them off scot-free. It's about my heart. It's about my response to the sacrifice of Jesus and doing as he did—

forgiving others. Forgiveness has the power to mend families, heal wounds, and help us to overcome our hurts, traumas, and abuses. It's why Jesus said, "But if you do not forgive others their sins, your Father will not forgive your sins." We can't be forgiven without first forgiving others. Yes, they harmed us. Yes, they caused us to lose faith in ourselves, others, and maybe even God, but forgiveness reconciles us with God. While we may never have the chance to confront the person or people who caused us pain (and it may not be advisable without proper guidance), forgiveness starts within and it is to be freely given. Even though we don't think our abusers deserve forgiveness, we have to remember that Jesus died for them, too

Chapter 11

I Choose to Forgive

I used to hate myself. It seemed that every choice I made was connected to me being a victim. I always felt dirty and not good enough. When you're raped by your stepdad over the course of 10 years starting as a preteen girl, you feel responsible for what's happening to you even though it isn't your fault. You're just there and you're an easy target for some lust-filled man who is bigger, stronger, and who can tell you that it's your fault and make you believe it. Every time he left my bed, I would replay it in my mind and wonder, *What if I would have screamed? … What if I would have hit him? … Would he have done this to me had I fought back?* I'll never know because I never tried. I felt too weak, too timid, and too afraid to fight back. Even when I tried screaming, nothing came out of my mouth. It felt like I was in a nightmare—the type where no matter how hard you try, you can't wake yourself up.

I've learned through my pain and what has happened to me has made me into who I need to be to help others like me.

It sounds crazy, but that one decision to forgive my rapist has made me thankful for having gone through it. God used my past hurts to allow me to see the purpose in my life. Now I get to be out there talking to teenagers and adults. I want to talk to people that feel like they're stuck, those that think that their life is never going to change. Women feeling like their challenges are too big to overcome. I want to teach them how to forgive and then how to start speaking up. I want them to know that when you lean on God, you can overcome anything. When you choose to forgive, you will become free. Yes, I still struggle with hurts from my past, some things you will carry with you for the rest of your life, but I also know that in Him, every day I get better.

And people cannot believe how far I've come in such a short time. I still pray for Rolf every day. Jesus died for him, too. I don't have thoughts like, *Oh my God. He's ruined this, and he's ruined that.* No. When I pray, I just pray that he finds peace. The first time I prayed for him, it was amazing. We all prayed for him and people asked whom it was that I was asking them to pray for. I told them that it was my rapist—and they were shocked.

I've since said many times that I've forgiven him or that I don't hate him anymore. There is power in prayer. I don't even know how to explain it, but I wish that more people would turn to God and say, "God, I need help. This is what I carry inside of me. Help me to forgive. I'm ready to take the power away from my past." If I can reach one person with this message and help them to get their life back, then I know I was successful. I've changed somebody's world.

* * *

"Then Peter came and said to Him, "Lord, how often shall my brother sin against me and I forgive him? Up to seven times?" Jesus said to him, "I do not say to you, up to seven times, but up to seventy times seven."

Matthew 18:21-22

Forgiveness is one of the most difficult teachings of Jesus. It has everything to do with the condition of our own hearts and less to do with letting someone off the hook. When I asked Jesus to forgive my sins, it's a very easy thing for me to do and for him to grant. He didn't remind me of all of the awful things I had done, the sins I had committed, and the ways that I had hurt him by how I lived my life. He just did it. And we are to do the same. Peter tried to get a hard and fast number of how many times to forgive and Jesus told him basically that it's a revolving door. Let's not mistake that as an invitation to let people walk over us, but that we are to forgive others and release them—and ourselves—from the prison of unforgiveness.

Once inside, Jesus does like any new tenant, he sweeps us clean and begins to redecorate our hearts to feel more like a home he would like to live in. He throws out the garbage of the past, opens the windows and our hearts, airs out from the bad smell of bitterness, and he makes our old hearts feel new, much like the decorators or renovators on one of those HGTV shows. We get a beautiful before and after if we trust him.

Coming to a point of learning how to forgive my rapist and reconcile with my family was a process. I wrestled with it. It was one of the most difficult things that I have ever had to do. I had to come to terms with a situation that I didn't ask for that turned my entire life upside down and created so much hurt for me. Everything I ever did in life up to the point of accepting Jesus I did out of that hurt, out of that bitterness, out of that pain. So, in learning to forgive the others, I had to forgive myself, too.

It's very hard teaching yourself to grasp and one that internally we resist. The reality is that forgiveness is really about us first. Forgiveness begins the process of opening our eyes and then our hearts. In the parable of the debtor, which Jesus shared after Peter's question on forgiveness, the king (God) allowed a debtor (me/you) to go free with a forgiven debt. Upon leaving prison with a clean slate and a zero-balance due, what did he do? He went straight to a man who owed him money and instead of forgiving the man's debt as the king forgave his debt, he had the man thrown into prison. When he heard of this, the king was not happy and in return judged him harshly. It will be the same for us if we cannot find in our hearts to forgive those who have been abusive to us, who have violated us, who have held us captive in fear through mental and physical abuse, and whatever else we have suffered at the hands of others. God forgives us freely despite what we have done and whether we deserve it or not, which we don't. He will not be able to forgive us if we don't respond to His grace by showing the same mercy to others.

This is probably something you cannot do on your own. I could not do it on my own. I turned to my pastors, I turned to my husband, and I turned to God. I wrestled with the idea of allowing people, who had hurt me so badly, to go free from the prison of hate that I had built for them. I will tell you that the minute I finally realized I needed to be united with God when it came to forgiveness, I began to feel free. This is why forgiveness is not only for us to give to other people, but for us to also give ourselves. What happened to me was not my fault and I had to forgive myself for thinking that I allowed it.

I want to encourage you to look at what the Bible says about forgiveness and find a way to forgive those who have wronged you. In talking to the Corinthian church about repentance, which is what happens when we forgive, Paul says the godly sorrow within us produces earnestness, it produces eagerness to clear ourselves, it produces indignation, and a readiness to see justice done. Letting go of the bitterness and hatred we feel and choosing to forgive creates a domino effect of wanting to make things right. For me, I prayed for those who harmed me. I was eager to let it go once I realized that God's love and protection would be there for me. That's what softened my heart.

One of the greatest testimonies of forgiveness was that of Jesus as he hung on the cross dying for our sins. At the foot of the cross, people insulted him, called him names, mocked him, and abused him. Yet despite it all, a man on the cross next to him asked for forgiveness and Jesus gave it to him on the spot. He also forgave the others at the foot of the cross. Can you imagine that? The Bible says, "But whoever has been forgiven little loves little." I chose to forgive because I was forgiven for so much.

Chapter 12

All a Part of God's Plan

My family seemed more involved in my life when I was a mess. Once I made the choice to sober up, clean up, speak up, and look up (to God), some of my relatives separated themselves from me. My close family in Germany—my brother, a couple of my uncles, some cousins, and people that were always in my life, are not as close to me now as they once were.

My brother and I have always had a strange relationship and it really wasn't a good one. Of course, we would have fun when we got together. But when I decided to write this book and began to speak up against the abuse I grew up with, my attempts to contact him, which had been almost daily, would go unanswered.

As for the rest of my family, they think that I've gone crazy. It makes me thank God for my kids and my husband, who are happy with the progress I have made since becoming a Christian. They have seen me in some really bad times and loved me through it. I suppose part of my family's opinion of my newfound faith is how they look at religion. In Germany, it's viewed differently than it is in the United States. Many Germans are either Catholic or Protestant and you don't find many young people in Germany attending church services like we do in the United States. I didn't grow up going to church, nor did anyone in my close family, unless there was a wedding or a baptism, which were all things based on tradition.

When I first started going to church with my husband and children, I began dealing with myself in a whole new way. Reading the Bible exposes you to who you really are and what's inside of your heart. Perhaps it's why some people don't want to go to church—dealing with our inner selves, our past, and our nature is hard. Studying the Bible changed me and because of that change, my family is distant, and they say negative things like I'm taking my commitment to God to a whole different level. But God changed me. What else would I do?

Changed lives scare family members and I understand that. They're seeing a side of me and of God that they don't know. In America, we're taught to draw close to God and that he's a loving God. In Germany, we were taught to fear God. He was seen as a strict parent who would make you suffer for everything you do wrong.

On the other side of that, some people in my family were saying that they're concerned about me and have asked if I was part of a cult. They don't believe a person can have a deep and meaningful relationship with Jesus, which leads to a life of joy, unless you're in a cult-type church, which is wrong. When I first began to seek God, even my mom was wondering what I was doing. She suggested I was going to attend church a couple of times and then stop because, after all, it was just a phase. She then proceeded to remind me of other phases I had in my life. It's been over two years and I don't miss a Sunday or a Wednesday unless I'm traveling out of town on business. Every time there is an event or an activity at the church, I'm there and I serve. I love going.

My mom realized that I was serious about God after seeing me go consistently for six or seven months; that's when she decided to come see it for herself. It was funny because since she grew up with such a different church experience, when we finished service, she said that she didn't feel like she went to church. I guess it was the contemporary music and the open expression of worship. It's not a quiet church at all, if you're used to quieter denominations. When she said it though, I took it as more of an insult. I was really hoping that she would turn to me and say, "Wow, this is refreshing," but no. She said, "It doesn't feel like church." She did come a second time to be sure that the church wasn't a cult. She met my pastors and other people in the congregation, and she thought they were all really nice.

She eventually warmed up to the idea of me being in church. During the weeks when we had our Newcomer's Lunch, she would cook some stuff and say, "Conny, take this to church with you. I made that for your Newcomer's Lunch." It blew me away because she could finally see how important God was to me and how much my life has changed. She understood that I didn't need to depend on alcohol and Valium to sooth my pain. She also realized that since I committed my life to Jesus, I hadn't been to a bar or club or had any alcohol, all of the things that distracted me from my real life before. She saw that what I was doing was good and positive for me and I think it is only a matter of time before she will follow Him, too. Once someone is willing to serve the church like she has been, even something as simple as making meals, that's the place where Jesus will begin to work on their heart.

* * *

"'Truly I tell you,' Jesus replied, 'no one who has left home or brothers or sisters or mother or father or children or fields for me and the gospel will fail to receive a hundred times as much in this present age: homes, brothers, sisters, mothers, children, and fields—along with persecutions—and in the age to come eternal life. But many who are first will be last, and the last first.'"

Mark 10:29-31

In this passage, Jesus teaches us who our family is in Him— our fellow believers. He's not dismissing our birth families, but for people like me who grew up with an unsupportive, dysfunctional, and broken family, Jesus reminds me that I can count on those who follow Him to be my family with God at the head. Despite my family thinking I was crazy for going all in on my relationship for Jesus, he says we who have left homes will receive a hundred times as much. The psalmist says, "God sets the lonely in families," and being actively involved in my church has helped me to feel wanted, loved, and accepted.

What happened with our birth families is they don't understand that to love Jesus is to have a closer relationship with him than with anyone else. When we come to faith, our family can feel slighted at what they perceive as us being overly loyal to perfect strangers who God has called our new spiritual family.

As I share and open up more of my life and my struggles with people in my church, and as we pray, we grow closer. Jesus connects us through prayer and through having a real and open relationship. These are things I didn't get in my natural family.

I have come to love my family more now because of Jesus. If it weren't for Christ, I would not be able to have the relationship with my mother that I have today. Our relationship had always been challenging and difficult, and sometimes very contentious, but now that I'm with Jesus, she gets to see firsthand his love working in my life, and how I've changed.

I still pray for my brother and my father that they will come to know God, as I now know him. I visited Germany for what I thought was a business trip last year, and, of course, God had a better plan for me. I was able to spend precious time with my parents and brother, which was so very much needed. They got to experience the new me: not drunk, not partying, and for once I didn't feel like I had to hide my feelings or my pain. I made myself available and answered all the questions my family had for so many years. True forgiveness has set in and all the blaming and finger-pointing has slowly turned into love, understanding, and support. As Christians, we should always have hope for those we love, no matter what. Despite my mom's failure to believe me, for many years, about my abuse, we now have a great relationship and a good understanding. Yes, we still have some ways to go before we all feel like a family again, but we are committed, and my family likes what Jesus has done for me. I'm grateful that Jesus has put me into a good church family. He will give you a family, too. I pray that when you seek a family, that you can find one in the body of Jesus Christ. He can give you people who stand with you, love you, and believe in you. You can have new brothers and sisters, new mothers and fathers, and as many children as you want to care for and serve. But it doesn't come without persecution. My family called me crazy. Even my mother thought there was something wrong with me when I became a Christian. They didn't want to believe I was a better version of myself, but I am. And your family may be the same way. Just follow Jesus, pray for those you love, and trust his plan.

Chapter 13

We Are Never Alone

All I wanted throughout my childhood was love, protection, and safety. Instead, I found myself in so many bad situations with no one to advocate for me. Unlike other children who grew up with aspirations, hopes, and dreams, I felt hopeless and lost. There was never a time when I said, "When I grow up, I'm going to be this or I'm going to be that," or "This is what I want to do with my life." I know that a child without some type of occupational dream seems odd, but I didn't have a typical childhood.

I discovered early in my life that I was good at listening and at helping other people manage their problems. I made myself available for my friends when they needed someone to talk to or when they fell on hard times. I liked trying to make a difference for people because it took me away from my problems; it distracted me from my pain and the abuse that was happening to me. Please don't mistake me as being selfish, I wanted to help because I love helping others, but I knew that if I were occupied with somebody else's drama, I wouldn't have to face my own.

It fills my heart the second I talk to somebody. Sometimes people come to me and open up about their problems. Once, the husband of a woman from my church had to go to the hospital. A spider had bitten him, and his muscles started to spasm. When she couldn't get ahold of a pastor, she called me, and then I met her at the hospital to pray with her. When I left the hospital, I was grateful and thankful that God had put this family in my life and allowed me to be there for them.

God choosing to use someone like me given all that has happened in my life is totally mind-blowing. It's amazing. I hope that I can even begin to bring people together to talking about their hurts, pain, and abuse, and to be able to start praying with them to show them how much is really possible with God because I see Him working in me and through me right now. My life is different now that I have totally surrendered and yours can be, too, just by allowing God to use you and your story. You will open yourself up to healing and in turn help someone just like you and me. It's a scary thing to do, but we are not alone and the more we raise our voices, the more God can work to restore the hearts of many.

I encourage you to start within and start with God. Then move into discipleship, counseling, and support groups within your church. You can't figure it out yourself, and you won't. You've seen what the fruits of my life were when I tried to do it on my own. Let God have it.

I've learned through all of this what it means to be open to the calling of God and when he puts someone on my heart, I'm obedient; I go and talk with them. I feel the need to reach out to others as much as I can. My husband, who finds it funny, said to me, "Love, trust in the voice. It's the Lord talking to you." It feels good to know that God wants to talk to me and can use me to help others. One of the best ways he's given me was social media.

When I started using Facebook as a tool for ministry to make videos to share with people, the first video I made was deeply personal. I had gone to a women's conference in Virginia Beach, Virginia. It just blew my mind listening to all of the powerful speakers. It was uplifting, motivating, and their stories inspired me to share my story. Until that day, I never felt like I could talk about the rape, abuse, and trauma I lived through publicly. I felt God telling me to just do it—in that moment—so I made a video and posted it on Facebook. It didn't hit me until later on when I thought, *Did you just really put that out there? Are you crazy? Have you lost your mind?*

The next day, I went to check on the video and it had over 600 views! I thought, *Oh my goodness! There's no sense in deleting that because everyone has already seen it.* So, I left it and people began texting and calling me to tell me they were inspired by it and that it helped them. I even had teenagers messaging me on Facebook. I had no idea who these young ladies were. But they all saw the video. One of them reached out to me, via a text message, expressing how I was the reason she gets out of bed every day. She said my video had a big impact on her life. That's when I knew it was the right thing to do, and so I kept making them.

Of course, there are those who do not appreciate the messages I send. Jesus did promise persecution. Other people have sent me messages, after seeing my videos, expressing concerns about their family members seeing the videos and acting upon my advice. I understand that, and the first time I got those sorts of messages, it concerned me. It caused me to wonder if what I was saying was helpful at all. I began to doubt. Then I remember that the same types of family members had shut me up when I'd tried to come forward with my story. Sexual abuse is an uncomfortable topic to hear, but a more uncomfortable truth to have to live with. Why do we protect the abuser at the expense of the victim? So, I continued to share my videos because I knew that there were people that I could help. I understand that I'm probably not going to help everybody, but if I just help one person, then I've done my job. I did what God put me here to do.

There was one young lady at work who was offended by my videos, so she reported me. She told my executive director (ED) that she thought I was mentally unstable and that I shouldn't have my job. She wondered what kind of message my videos sent out to the families who came to our workplace. I was summoned for a meeting in the manager's office. During our meeting, I told the manager and the ED that this message had to be shared and I was the one to share it. I also told them they would have to fire me because I wasn't going to stop. They didn't fire me, however, I decided to resign not long afterward. God was leading me in a direction that I wanted to follow. We were changing lives together—Him through me. I just believe in the work of God, in my life, to save others from cycles of pain, PTSD, trauma, and abuse. You just have to believe in yourself.

We can and will overcome if we continue to pray, walk with Jesus, and let him work in our lives.

I can say, though, that I definitely have received more encouraging messages, texts, and phone calls than I have negative ones. My family in Germany is probably the most negative about it. They're not comfortable with who I am in God now. They prefer the woman who didn't say anything—the woman who refused to stand up for herself. The woman in the drunken state running the streets and doing everything she wasn't supposed to do. That person is gone. This is my story, but it's not really my story for me, it's my story for so many. Women like you perhaps, or someone you love. I need people who have suffered in silence from abuse to see there is a good life out there.

No matter what, I've learned that focusing on Jesus and staying true to my calling makes me feel grateful. I will keep sharing my videos and inspiring more people to come forward to be healed from the wounds of their abusive pasts and I won't back down.

* * *

"Do nothing out of selfish ambition or vain conceit. Rather, in humility value others above yourselves, not looking to your own interests but each of you to the interests of the others."

Philippians 2:2-4

Purpose is found in Jesus. My story could have continued to be one without purpose, value. I had no goals for myself; I didn't believe my life had any value in it whatsoever. As a result, I did drugs, abused alcohol, was promiscuous, was disrespectful, and had an attitude of someone who just did not care. My hurts compounded over years. I had no one in my life that cared about me. When I would reach out to my mother to talk about some of the things that happened to me, she thought that I was crazy. My family members thought that I was crazy, too, because I was acting out and running wild in the streets. No one had a vision for my life. Over time, I learned to accept that I was going nowhere. It's not something that just happened overnight, but it was all the hurts, the pain, and the disappointment that I had to endure. The one thing that never left me though was a sense of compassion toward other people. I was good at listening to my friends and helping them solve their problems. It helped me to ignore my own.

Finding God was a game changer for me. Sometimes I wonder what took me so long. It wasn't until I started to become more vocal about the abuse that I suffered that I really saw the work of God. When I decided to write this book, to talk about those past hurts and pains and all the things that came with those, it bothered a lot of people. I can't help that though. Jesus bothered a lot of people, too, and the result was that many people escaped God's wrath.

Paul admonished Timothy, saying that God who started out with a good work would carry it to completion. As I look at my life, I believe that. Despite being sexually, physically, and mentally abused, I see it now as the work of God. No, I'm not saying that God delights in seeing people suffer. I was abused and hurt, but also given a warm spirit, resilient character, and a listening ear for a greater purpose. I firmly believe that. Now, I have a story to tell. You have a story to tell, too—a good work that needs to be carried out. Don't hide it anymore. Don't protect your abusers and rapists anymore. Don't keep their secrets anymore.

When I decided to make that first video, I was scared to death, but I did it anyway. I thought of women like you who are reading this book looking for someone else just like you to confirm that you're not alone. I did it for people who felt no one believed them; for those whose families were like mine and dismissed the notion of abuse. I know what you're feeling. I know it well. Those videos were never just about my abuse or me. I wasn't looking for sympathy. I wasn't looking for people to send me messages saying, "Oh, you poor thing." I was looking to take the little bit of courage that God put in my heart that day to say clearly that rape and abuse are no longer acceptable. I was tired of being quiet about it and wanted to use my voice and my life to be an encouragement to those who needed it. God wanted me to show my face in a public forum to say that we no longer have to hide. And every day, He reminds me as He prompts me to speak to this person or that or to post this status or that video that in Christ I have a powerful ally. I'll never have to walk this journey alone—and if you trust Him, neither will you.

Conclusion

Making the decision to forgive my stepdad, my mother, my abusive ex-husbands, and ultimately myself wasn't easy. As I traded in the hurts that I held so tightly for the freedom only found in a relationship with Jesus Christ, the gift of forgiveness has taught me that there is nothing more comforting than knowing I can hand my heart to Jesus. In him, I have hope and light. Thinking that I was alone with my pain, stuck in dark places, and that I may never find a way out is what kept me on those roller coasters of nightmares, anger, and shame. After choosing to forgive, my heart was touched in ways I still can't fully describe. I can only compare it to the feeling of meeting my very first crush, and how the butterflies that were flying around my tummy are now touching my heart. I have now experienced love and life in a different way.

Choosing to forgive also meant letting go of guilt and shame. Jesus gave me the courage to take responsibility for my actions. For the first time in my life, I am able to tell the world who I really am—no more lies. Jesus told me, "If God is for you, who can be against you." He was holding my hand every step of the way. I just didn't know it. I was guilty in so many ways but was forgiven this whole time, I just didn't realize it. I was made new and received a fresh start free of the baggage and bad feelings that held me down all these years.

I went from thinking I was not good enough to all things are possible. The people I was so afraid of losing are closer to me than ever. Yes, you will find that some people are not ready for the new you and may never be ready, but that's OK. We are all on our own journey and have to make tough decisions. All I can tell you is decisions that seemed so very hard before became easier with every step of the way through forgiveness.

I know that you may not be in the same place I am now, but you are where I was. I want to encourage you to get open about your pain. Carrying around this burden only gets more difficult as time passes. As I've shared my journey, I found out that I am not alone; there are so many of us. I've helped young girls, women, and families. By sharing my story with them, they realized that we don't have to be stuck in this miserable place forever, all it takes is us putting our faith in God—yes, it really is that easy. I thought that I would never have the same bond with my brother and mother as I did as a little girl, but a recent trip to Germany proved me wrong. As I forgave myself and took responsibility, I gained the trust, love, and support from my family, which means the world to me. My brother was always my hero when I was little, but with me being distant and stuck in a dark place, we grew apart. My family accepts me for the Christian that I am. I have a wonderful relationship with my mom now. We have long talks about God and his word. I understand why the people I love so much couldn't be a part of my journey. I had to find Jesus. Nobody can knock on that door for you and nobody can ask the questions for you. You have to seek to find. I promise you, Jesus is right behind that door in front of you; all you have to do is knock.

I hope that my story inspired you, gave you courage, and helped you to realize that you don't have to hide anymore. We are all perfectly flawed but perfectly loved by God. I leave you with this Scripture and a prayer. I hope you'll be the next to join me in disturbing the silence.

> *"'For I know the plans I have for you,' says the Lord.*
> *'They are plans for good and not for disaster, to give you*
> *a future and hope.'"*

> Jeremiah 29:11

Dear God,

Thank you for loving us unconditionally with all of our flaws. Thank you for giving me the courage to share my story and blessing me every day with life, trust, and hope. I am asking you, dear God, to mend the broken the way you have mended me. Let my story give courage to those who so desperately need it. I pray that every single person that is reading this right now will feel your presence, your touch of comfort, and everlasting love. Heavenly Father, I am asking you to give each and every one of us life without anxiety, addiction, fear, shame, and guilt, bless us with strength to step out of our comfort zones and put on the armor you provide us with every single day. I pray this in your mighty name.

Amen.

Notes

All Scripture and references, in order of appearance in the book, are quoted from the New International Version unless otherwise stated.

Foreword
- "…the substance of things hoped for, and the evidence of things not seen." Hebrews 11:1(KJV)
- "…to comfort those in any trouble with the comfort we ourselves receive from God." 2 Corinthians 1:4

Introduction
- "This is my comfort in my affliction, that your word has revived me." Psalm 119:50 (NASB)
- "When [The Pharisees] saw the courage of Peter and John and realized that they were unschooled, ordinary men, they were astonished and they took note that these men had been with Jesus." Acts 4:23

Chapter 1

- "If anyone causes one of these little ones—those who believe in me—to stumble, it would be better for them if a large millstone were hung around their neck and they were thrown into the sea." Mark 9:42
- "Hosanna to the Son of David! Blessed is he who comes in the name of the Lord!" Matthew 21:9
- "He is the God who avenges me, who subdues nations under me." Psalm 18:47

Chapter 2

- "When Jesus climbed out of the boat, a man possessed by an evil spirit came out from a cemetery to meet him… Day and night he wandered among the burial caves and in the hills, howling and cutting himself with sharp stones." Mark 5:2,5 NLT
- "Praise be to the God and Father of our Lord Jesus Christ, the Father of compassion and the God of all comfort, who comforts us in all our troubles, so that we can comfort those in any trouble with the comfort we ourselves receive from God. For just as we share abundantly in the sufferings of Christ, so also our comfort abounds through Christ." 2 Corinthians 1:3-5
- The Scriptures promise time and again that if we seek him we will find him (1 Chronicles 28:9, 2 Chronicles 15:2, Acts 17:27)

Chapter 3

- "In the course of time, Amnon son of David fell in love with Tamar, the beautiful sister of Absalom son of David. Amnon became so obsessed with his sister Tamar that he made himself ill. She was a virgin, and it seemed impossible for him to do anything to her" 2 Samuel 13: 1-2
- "Amnon hated her with intense hatred. In fact, he hated her more than he had loved her." 2 Samuel 13:15

Chapter 4

- "Suppose one of you has a hundred sheep and loses one of them. Doesn't he leave the ninety-nine in the open country and go after the lost sheep until he finds it?" Luke 15:4
- "The Lord is not slow in keeping his promise, as some understand slowness. Instead he is patient with you, not wanting anyone to perish, but everyone to come to repentance." 2 Peter 3:9

Chapter 5

- "Or do you not know that your body is a temple of the Holy Spirit within you, whom you have from God? You are not your own, for you were bought with a price. So glorify God in your body." 1 Corinthians 6:19-20 (ESV)
- "Cast all your anxiety on him because he cares for you." 1 Peter 5:7

Chapter 6

- "Therefore, if anyone is in Christ, the new creation has come: The old has gone, the new is here!" 2 Corinthians 5:17

Chapter 7

- "David noticed that his attendants were whispering among themselves, and he realized the child was dead. 'Is the child dead?' he asked. 'Yes,' they replied, 'he is dead.'" 2 Samuel 12:19
- "I will go to him, but he will not return to me." 2 Samuel 12:23
- "The Lord is close to the brokenhearted and saves those who are crushed in spirit." Psalm 34:18
- "After Job had prayed for his friends, the Lord restored his fortunes and gave him twice as much as he had before. All his brothers and sisters and everyone who had known him before came and ate with him in his house. They comforted and consoled him over all the trouble the Lord had brought on him, and each one gave him a piece of silver and a gold ring. The Lord blessed the latter part of Job's life more than the former part. He had fourteen thousand sheep, six thousand camels, a thousand yoke of oxen, and a thousand donkeys. And he also had seven sons and three daughters." Job 42:10

Chapter 8

- "Follow my example, as I follow the example of Christ." 1 Corinthians 1:11
- "To this you were called, because Christ suffered for you, leaving you an example that you should follow in his steps." 1 Peter 2:21

Chapter 9

• "As it is written in Isaiah the prophet: I will send my messenger ahead of you, who will prepare your way—a voice of one calling in the wilderness, 'Prepare the way for the Lord, make straight paths for him.' And so John the Baptist appeared in the wilderness, preaching a baptism of repentance for the forgiveness of sins." Mark 1:2-4

Chapter 10

• "This is what you are to say to Joseph: 'I ask you to forgive your brothers the sins and the wrongs they committed in treating you so badly.' Now please forgive the sins of the servants of the God of your father. When their message came to him, Joseph wept." Genesis 50:17

• "Before the years of famine came, two sons were born to Joseph by Asenath daughter of Potiphera, priest of On. Joseph named his firstborn Manasseh and said, 'It is because God has made me forget all my trouble and all my father's household.' The second son he named Ephraim and said, 'It is because God has made me fruitful in the land of my suffering.'" Genesis 41:50-52

• "But if you do not forgive others their sins, your Father will not forgive your sins." Matthew 6:15

Chapter 11

• "Then Peter came and said to Him, "Lord, how often shall my brother sin against me and I forgive him? Up to seven times?" Jesus said to him, "I do not say to you, up to seven times, but up to seventy times seven." Matthew 18:21-22

- Jesus' Parable on Forgiveness (Matthew 18:23-35)
- Paul on Godly Sorrow (2 Corinthians 7:9-11)
- "But whoever has been forgiven little loves little." Luke 7:47

Chapter 12

- "'Truly I tell you,' Jesus replied, 'no one who has left home or brothers or sisters or mother or father or children or fields for me and the gospel will fail to receive a hundred times as much in this present age: homes, brothers, sisters, mothers, children, and fields—along with persecutions— and in the age to come eternal life. But many who are first will be last, and the last first.'" Mark 10:29-31
- Psalm 68:6

Chapter 13

- "Do nothing out of selfish ambition or vain conceit. Rather, in humility value others above yourselves, not looking to your own interests but each of you to the interests of the others." Philippians 2:2-4
- Paul encourages Timothy (Philippians 1:6)

Epilogue

- Personalized from "If God is for us, who can be against us?" Romans 8:31
- "'For I know the plans I have for you,' says the Lord. 'They are plans for good and not for disaster, to give you a future and hope.'" Jeremiah 29:11 (NLT)

Acknowledgements

First and foremost, I would like to thank Pastor Craig a.k.a. P.C. and his wonderful wife Lezli of Upward Church, as well as Pastor David and his wife, Stacy. In the darkest hours, you guys introduced me to Jesus and helped me find the light. The days I wanted to give up you lifted me up, prayed, and cried with me. Thank you!

To Chris Jones: I will be forever grateful that God introduced us. I want you to know that you made a big difference in my family's life. You didn't just help me with Mended Faith but became that one person that I trusted with my secret and my life.

To Pastor Jerry Jude: I felt each and every prayer of encouragement from you through this process.

To my children: We have been through so much together. I thank you for giving me a chance to be the mom God has always wanted me to be.

To Lawrence: In the darkest hours, you prayed and supported me with the help of Jesus. You have saved my life. You are truly heaven-sent.

To Mom: It's been a journey and I want you to know that I understand. Your support means the world to me. There is nothing you could have done to prevent the things that happened. This was all part of a plan that we may not always understand but must trust that God knows what he is doing. I pray that you will find the same forgiveness that I have found.

To Dad: I did listen to everything you taught me. Thank you for being here for me always.

To Hans-Dieter: I know it wasn't easy to like me during my dark and shameful moments. It means the world to me to have your support and love. #DisturbTheSilence

To my church family: Thank you for being the best family one could ever ask for. #Freedom

To my editor, Maude Campbell, I thank you.

To my publisher, Morgan James Publishing. Thank you for making this book a reality.

About Cornelia Jude

Cornelia Jude is an entrepreneur, wife, and mother of six. Born and raised in Germany, she moved to the United States in 1997 and became a citizen in 2010.

As a doTERRA Silver Advocate, Cornelia has built an impressive downline in just over a year with 184 wellness advocates spanning 18 states and eight countries. Helping people find holistic health and wellness solutions through essential oils is a contagious passion of hers.

Despite enduring years of sexual, physical, and mental abuse, which led to a 1999 PTSD diagnosis, Cornelia fights every day to live her life as a survivor and not a victim! After embracing the Christian faith in 2016, she has come to terms with the pain of her past and looks forward to the plans that God has for her future. Her goal is to share with others how she turned her most painful memories into something positive through the strength of Christ. She achieves this through sharing her business with others and connecting with nearly 3,000 engaged fans, friends, and followers on her Facebook pages.

Cornelia lives in Virginia with her husband, Lawrence, and their children.

About Chris Jones

Chris Jones is a three-time award-winning journalist and editor, and the author of The Art & Business of Writing: A Practical Guide to the Writing Life. He hosts The Art & Business of Writing podcast, a weekly show where he interviews writers, authors, and creative professionals who influence the writing world. Some of his guests have  included New York Times bestselling author John David Mann, USA Today bestselling author Joanna Penn, EOFire's Kate Erickson, and Foundr Magazine publisher Nathan Chan. Chris lives in Virginia with his wife, Elizabeth, and their children.

Morgan James
Speakers Group

➢ www.TheMorganJamesSpeakersGroup.com

We connect Morgan James published
authors with live and online events
and audiences who will benefit
from their expertise.

Morgan James makes all of our titles available
through the Library for All Charity Organization.

www.LibraryForAll.org